BASIC GEOMETRY

COPYRIGHT © 1999 Mark Twain Media, Inc.

ISBN 1–58037–105–1

Printing No. CD–1332

Mark Twain Media, Inc., Publishers
Distributed by Carson-Dellosa Publishing Company, Inc.

    The purchase of this book entitles the buyer to reproduce the student pages for classroom use only. Other permissions may be obtained by writing Mark Twain Media, Inc., Publishers.

All rights reserved. Printed in the United States of America.

TABLE OF CONTENTS

Introduction iv

Points—Lines—Planes 1
    Introduction 1
    Undefined Terms 1
    Point 2
    Line Segment 2
    Straight Line 3
    Relationships Between Points and Lines 3
    Collinear Points 4
    Ray 5
    Plane 6
    Relationships of Points, Lines, and Planes 7
    Coplanar Lines and Skew Lines 9
    Intersections of Lines and Planes 10
    Angle 11
    Polygon 12
    Triangle 12
    Quadrilateral 13
    Other Polygons 13
    Polygonal Regions 14
    Symbols for Geometric Figures 14
    Exercises 15
    Discovery Exercise 17

Congruence 19
    Pretest Exercises 19
    Congruence and Equality 23
    Congruent Line Segments 24
    Congruent Angles 24
    Right Angles 24
    Classification of Triangles and Quadrilaterals 25
    Relationships of Quadrilaterals 26
    Regular Polygons 27
    Circle 27
    Arc 28
    Symbols 28
    Exercises 29
    Visual Aid for Geometry 35
    Area Activity 36

Concave and Convex Figures 38
    Convex Figures 38
    Concave Figures 39
    Exercises 40

Basic Geometry

TABLE OF CONTENTS

Lines of Symmetry **41**
    Line Symmetry 41
    Exercises 43

Measurement of Angles **44**
    Degrees 44
    Special Names for Angles According to Their Measures 46
    Complementary and Supplementary Angles 46
    Exercises 47

Constructions **56**
    Intersection Exercises 57
    Construct a Line Segment Congruent to a Given Segment 58
    Bisect a Line Segment 58
    Construct a Ray Perpendicular to a Line at a Given Point in a Line 60
    Construct a Perpendicular From a Point to a Line 61
    Bisect a Given Angle 63
    Construct an Angle Congruent to a Given Angle 65
    Construct a Triangle Congruent to a Given Triangle 66
    Construct a Line Through a Given Point and Parallel to a Given Line 66
    Construct a Line Parallel to a Given Line and at a Given Distance From It 67
    Separate a Circle Into Six Congruent Arcs 69
    Constructions Exercises 70
    Geometric Patterns and Addition 77
    Paper Folding 79

Space Figures **84**
    Prisms 86
        Patterns for Prisms 88
    Pyramids 92
        Patterns for Pyramids 92
    Cylinders 95
        Pattern for Cylinder 96
    Spheres 97
    Volumes and Surface Areas for Specific Figures 100
        Exercises 106
    The Five Regular Polyhedrons 108
        Tetrahedron 109
        Octahedron 110
        Icosahedron 111
        Hexahedron (Cube) 112
        Dodecahedron 113

Glossary **114**

Answer Keys **119**

INTRODUCTION

Basic Geometry provides instruction and activity sheets on the concepts that are the basis for all geometry. The student will be led from the fundamental notion of a point all the way through a ray and line; from an angle through transversals; and from two-dimensional objects through three-dimensional objects.

All basic geometry concepts are covered. The student will learn how to determine supplementary and complementary angles. The relationships formed by adjacent angles, alternate interior angles, vertical angles, and so on are also examined. Classification of triangles and quadrilaterals is presented in detail. Ultimately, the student will experience three-dimensional objects and learn how to classify them and figure their volumes and surface areas. Patterns are provided to give the students opportunities for hands-on construction of several three-dimensional objects.

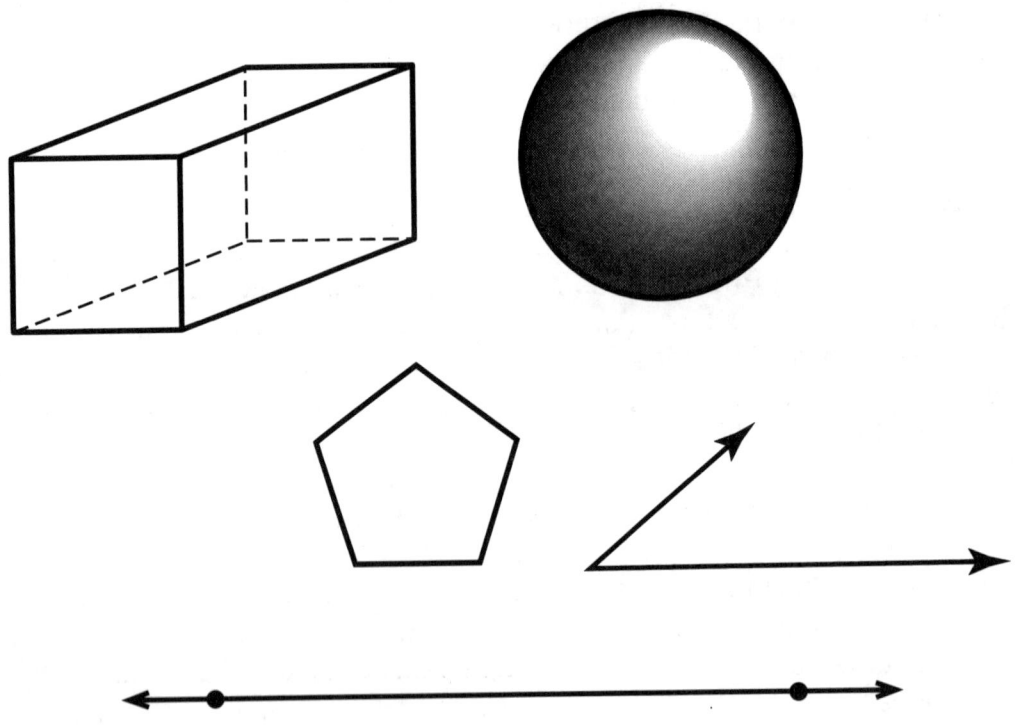

POINTS—LINES—PLANES

Introduction

Points and lines are the building blocks of geometry. Points, lines, planes, plane figures, and solids are abstract concepts. The pictures drawn on paper are models of these abstract concepts. For example, a straight mark made along the edge of a ruler is not a line, but a picture of part of a line. The mark made by the pencil of a compass is not a circle but a picture of a circle.

Drawings and constructions in geometry are representations of geometric ideas. They are not the ideas themselves. However, language tends to become monotonous when such directions as "draw a picture of a circle," "draw a model of a line," "draw a picture of a triangle," and so on, are used. For this reason, and because "draw" implies "picture," some authors merely say "draw a circle," "draw a line," "draw a triangle," and so on.

An important objective of mathematics programs is to develop terminology and to present ideas in such a way that students will not have things to "unlearn" in later courses. For example, color the circle and the rectangle below.

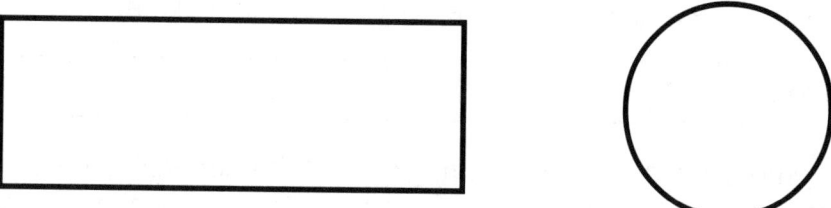

Did you color the inside of each figure or did you merely trace the boundary? Is the center of a circle a point of the circle? Some agreement is needed as to what is meant by "rectangle" and by "circle." These two examples are intended to illustrate the reason why greater precision in language is advocated.

Undefined Terms

Points, lines, and planes are usually undefined terms in elementary school geometry. The definition of any given word in the dictionary is defined in terms of other words. If each of these words in turn is defined, eventually the original word will appear in one of the definitions. Hence the set of definitions is circular. In mathematics, such circularity is avoided by agreeing not to define certain terms.

Basic Geometry　　　　　　　　　　　　　POINTS—LINES—PLANES: Point/Line Segment

Point

In modern geometry a point is an undefined concept about which intuitive notions may be established. The tip of a needle when the needle is in a fixed location may represent a point in space. When the needle is moved, the tip suggests another point.

The tip of the needle may be moved, but not the mathematical point. A mathematical point is a fixed location. It cannot be moved.

A point may be represented by drawing a dot on paper. The dot, however, is not a mathematical point. It merely suggests a point. To distinguish different points represented by dots, capital letters are used. The five points represented by dots below are designated as A, B, C, D, and E. When a single capital letter is used, it will represent a point.

B .
　　　　　　　　　　　　D .
　　　　C .　　　　　　　　　　　E .
A .

Space may be considered as the set of all points or locations. In geometry, subsets of the set of points of space are considered. Examples of such subsets are a single point, the set of points in a line segment, and the set of points in a plane.

Line Segment

A line segment is a set of points. Imagine that the dotted line below is a picture of some of the points in a line segment. Then imagine that a point can be located between each two successive points and that this can be continued indefinitely. Between each pair of points there is another point.

....

Below are two points A and B. The dots and not the capital letters represent the points. (This is not always clear to children.) Use your ruler and make a straight mark to connect the two dots. Then imagine that this mark is the set of all points between A and B together with the points A and B.

A .　　　　　　　　　　　　　　　　　　　　　　　　　　　　　. B

The union of the two points A and B and the set of points between A and B is line segment AB. A line segment has two endpoints. The endpoints of segment AB are A and B. The symbol "$\overline{AB}$" is used to designate this particular segment. The symbol "$\overline{AB}$" is read as "line segment AB" or just "segment AB" for short. To name a line segment, two capital letters with a bar above them to suggest a segment are used.

Now make a second straight mark to connect the points A and B above. How many straight marks can you make to connect these two points? _____

When a second mark is made from point A to point B, it is merely a retracing of the first mark. This suggests that one and only one segment can have A and B as endpoints. If the mark through A and B is extended to the edges of the paper, any other mark through A and B is merely a retracing of the first mark. The length of the mark is limited by the extent of the sheet of paper, but it is easy to imagine a mark that is unlimited in extent. This leads to the notion of a straight line.

Straight Line

A geometric straight line is unlimited in extent. It has no endpoints. A line is another undefined term in geometry, but a mark made along the edge of a ruler suggests the notion of a line. When the word *line* is used, it will be understood to mean "straight line." A line is often represented as a double arrow, indicating that it extends without limit in both directions.

However, some authors picture a line this way.

To name a line, any two points in the line may first be selected and named by capital letters. For example, both lines pictured above may be named "line AB" or by the symbol "$\overleftrightarrow{AB}$." The symbol "$\overleftrightarrow{AB}$" is read "line AB." Notice that the double arrow above the two capital letters suggests one way of representing a line.

Relationships Between Points and Lines

Below is a single point Q. How many lines can be drawn through Q? Use your ruler to find the answer to this question. Lines that contain the same point are said to be concurrent.

A single point may be contained in an unlimited number of lines.

Basic Geometry POINTS—LINES—PLANES: Relationships Between Points and Lines/Collinear Points

If two lines intersect, they have only one point in common. In the illustration the lines $\overleftrightarrow{AB}$ and $\overleftrightarrow{CD}$ intersect at a point E. $\overleftrightarrow{AB} \cap \overleftrightarrow{CD} = \{E\}$

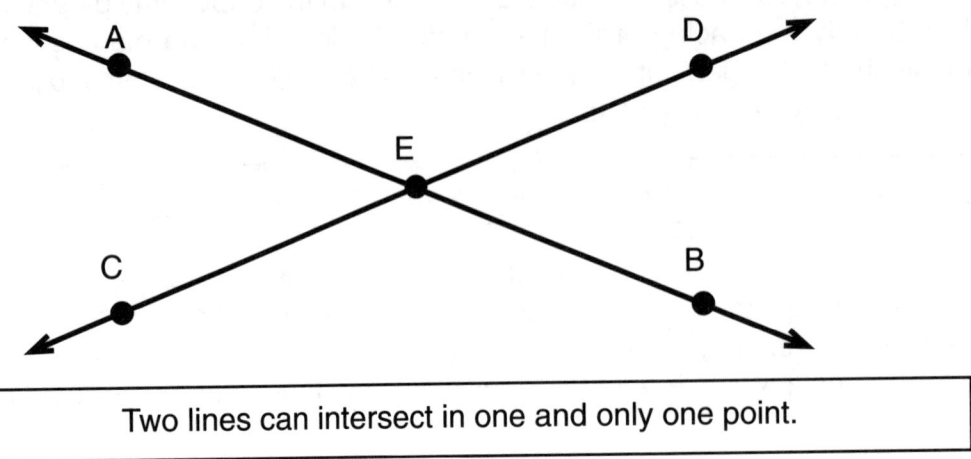

Two lines can intersect in one and only one point.

Two different points determine a line. Only one straight mark representing a line may be made through two dots representing points. Any other mark is a retracing of the first mark. That only one line contains the two distinct points A and B is illustrated below.

Two distinct points can be contained in one and only one line.

Collinear Points

If three points are located so that one is between the other two, the three points are said to be **collinear**. "Betweenness" is considered a property only of points in a line. Thus collinear points will always lie in a straight line. In the illustration A, B, and C lie in $\overleftrightarrow{AC}$ and represent collinear points. The point B is between A and C.

Three points not in the same straight line are said to be **noncollinear** points since there is no "betweenness" property. A, B, and C in the illustration below are noncollinear points. No point is between the other two. Notice that three noncollinear points determine three lines.

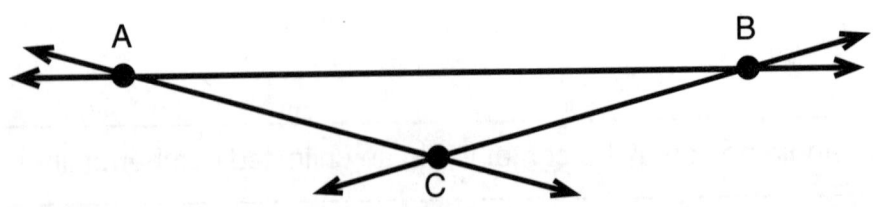

Basic Geometry

POINTS—LINES—PLANES: Ray

Ray

Any one point P in a line divides the set of points in the line into two half lines. Point P does not belong to either half line. In the illustration, the union of the point P and the set of points in the half line to the right of P is a set of points called a ray. Likewise, the union of P and all the points in the half line to the left of P is another set of points called a ray. A ray has only one endpoint.

To designate a ray, a second point of the ray may be named. The two rays pictured in the illustration below are named $\overrightarrow{OA}$ and $\overrightarrow{OB}$. The first capital letter names the one endpoint of the ray, and the second capital letter some other point on the ray. An arrow above two capital letters is the distinguishing symbol for a ray. The symbol "$\overrightarrow{OA}$" is read "ray OA". (In later mathematics this symbol, two capital letters with an arrow above them, may also be used to represent a vector.)

Each line contains an unlimited number of rays. In the illustration below, identify each of the following rays: $\overrightarrow{AE}$, $\overrightarrow{EA}$, $\overrightarrow{AB}$, $\overrightarrow{CA}$, $\overrightarrow{ED}$.

Notice that $\overrightarrow{AB}$ is the same ray as $\overrightarrow{AC}$, $\overrightarrow{AD}$, and $\overrightarrow{AE}$. Also notice that $\overrightarrow{ED}$ is the same ray as $\overrightarrow{EC}$, $\overrightarrow{EB}$, and $\overrightarrow{EA}$.

Plane

A plane is another undefined mathematical term. The set of points in a plane, like a point and the set of points in a line, has no physical existence. A plane is an abstract concept.

The flat surface of a table top suggests a portion of a plane. Imagine that the surface of the table top is extended in all directions. This imaginary unlimited flat surface may be considered as a representation of the set of points in a plane. Planes, like lines, are unlimited in extent. Other representations of parts of planes may include the walls, floor, and ceiling of a room.

Imagine all the dots that could be made on a sheet of paper, and then imagine each dot as a point in a part of a plane. A plane is an unlimited set of points.

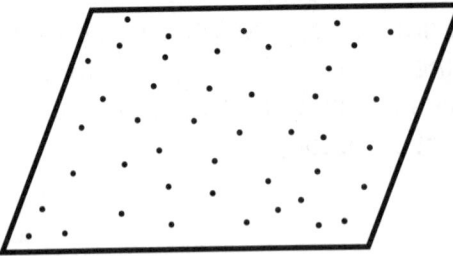

Next imagine all the different line segments that may be represented on the sheet of paper and then imagine these segments as lines.

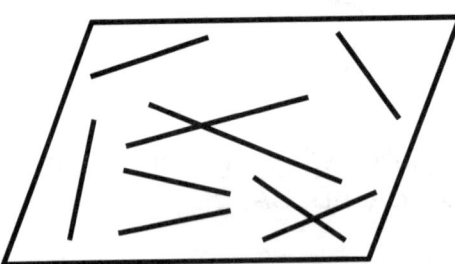

A plane contains an unlimited number of points, an unlimited number of line segments, an unlimited number of lines, an unlimited number of rays, and so on.

Usually a plane is represented as in the illustration and may be named in several different ways. It may be named by using one, two, three, or four letters or by a letter in a script font. In this discussion, a plane will be designated by a script letter. The plane illustrated may be designated as $\mathscr{P}$.

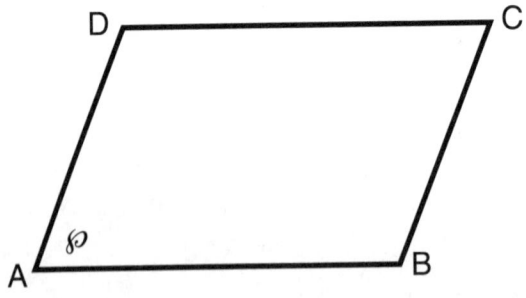

Relationships of Points, Lines, and Planes

Mark two dots A and B on a sheet of paper. Make a straight mark through the two dots. The mark may be thought of as a picture of a line in a plane. If any two different points in a plane are located, these two points determine a line. This suggests that:

> If two different points are in a plane, then the line determined by these points is in that same plane.

In other words, if two different points of a line are in a given plane, then the entire line is a subset of that plane. The illustration below shows a line AB in a plane $\Re$.

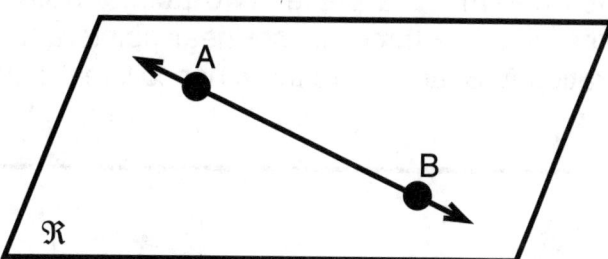

Two points are contained in an unlimited number of planes. Likewise, the line determined by these two points is contained in an unlimited number of planes. The illustration below represents three planes containing points A and B and hence $\overleftrightarrow{AB}$.

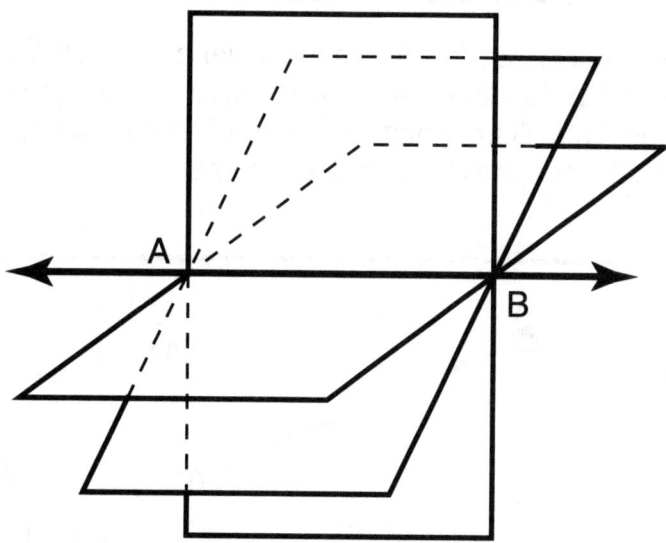

It is easy to imagine other planes containing A and B. This suggests that:

> An unlimited number of planes contain any two distinct points and the line determined by these two points.

A third relationship between points and a plane may be illustrated by spreading your thumb, index finger, and middle finger to support a book. The book rests firmly on the three fingers.

A three-legged stool does not wobble, while a badly made four-legged table will not stand firmly. Why? Three noncollinear points are always in the same plane, while four points may not all be in the same plane.

> Any three noncollinear points determine one and only one plane.

When the above property is assumed for a plane, two other relationships may be deduced.

Two intersecting lines determine a plane. Two points in one line and a third noncollinear point in the other line are three noncollinear points and thus determine a plane. In the following illustration A, B, and C are three noncollinear points that determine a plane.

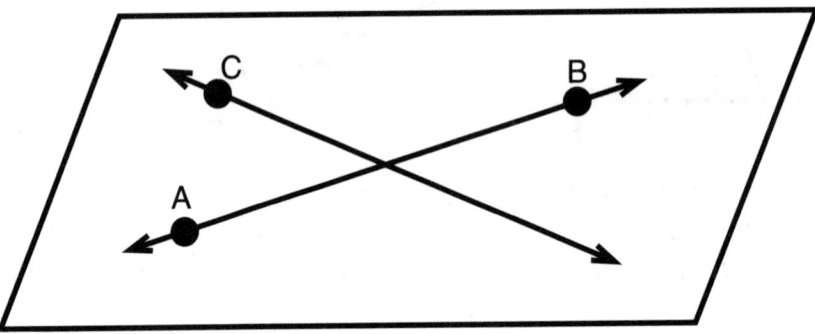

A line and a point not in that line determine a plane. Two different points in the same line and a third point not in that line are three noncollinear points and thus determine a plane. In the illustration A and B are points in $\overleftrightarrow{AB}$ and C is a third point not collinear with A and B. The three noncollinear points determine a plane.

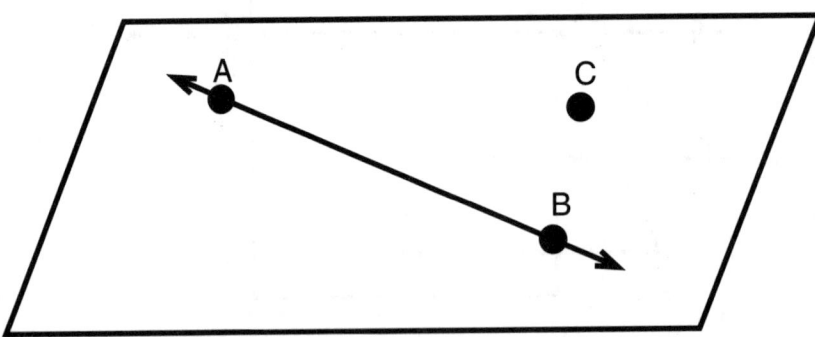

Basic Geometry POINTS—LINES—PLANES: Coplanar Lines and Skew Lines

Coplanar Lines and Skew Lines

If two lines are in the same plane, they are called **coplanar** lines. Any two coplanar lines either intersect or are parallel. Conversely, if two lines are parallel or if they intersect, they are coplanar.

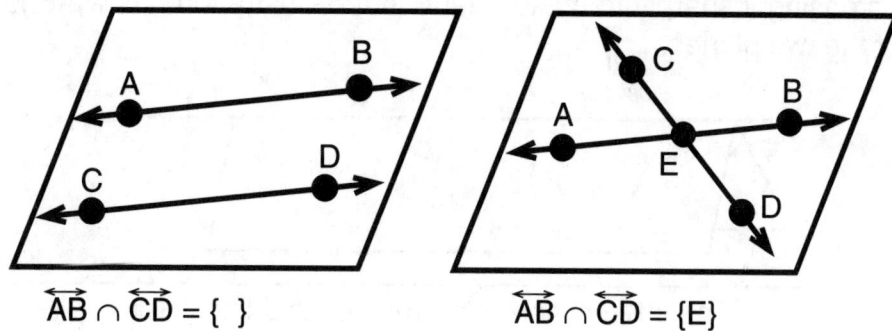

$\overleftrightarrow{AB} \cap \overleftrightarrow{CD} = \{\ \}$ $\overleftrightarrow{AB} \cap \overleftrightarrow{CD} = \{E\}$

Parallel lines are coplanar lines that do not intersect. In set language, two coplanar lines are parallel if their intersection is the empty set.

Subsets of parallel lines are also said to be parallel. The following illustration shows two parallel segments, two parallel rays, and a line, a ray, and a line segment that are parallel.

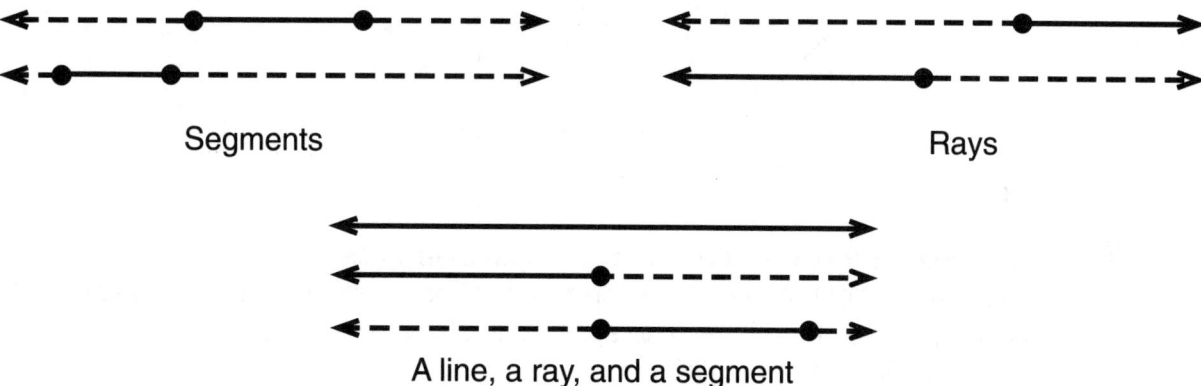

Segments   Rays

A line, a ray, and a segment

Two lines that are not coplanar are called **skew lines**. Such lines are neither parallel nor do they intersect. In the illustration below $\overleftrightarrow{AB}$ and $\overleftrightarrow{CD}$ are skew lines.

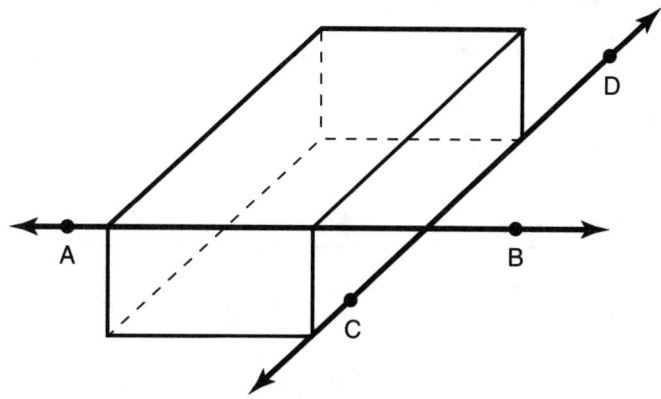

© Mark Twain Media, Inc., Publisher   9

Intersections of Lines and Planes

Two planes either intersect or they are parallel. Two adjacent sidewalls of a room are representations of planes that intersect. The **intersection** of two planes is a line.

The intersection of two planes may also be represented by folding in halves a sheet of paper and creasing it sharply to make a tent. In the illustration below $\overleftrightarrow{AB}$ is the line of intersection of the two planes.

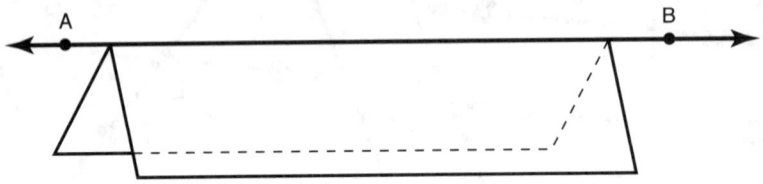

The intersection of two planes is a line.

Two planes that do not intersect are said to be **parallel**. In set language, two planes are parallel if their intersection is the empty set. In the illustration below, $\wp$ and $\Re$ are parallel planes. $\wp \cap \Re = \{\ \}$.

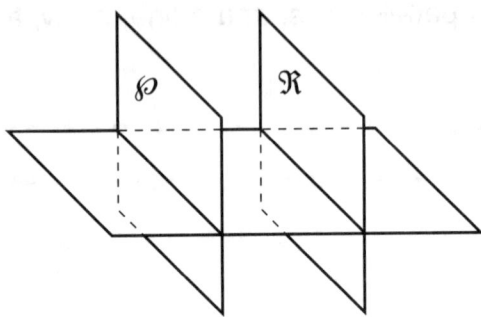

If a line intersects a plane, then either the line intersects the plane at one point or the whole line is a subset of the plane. The first illustration shows several lines, each with all of its points contained in the plane. The second illustration below shows several lines, each intersecting the plane at a single point.

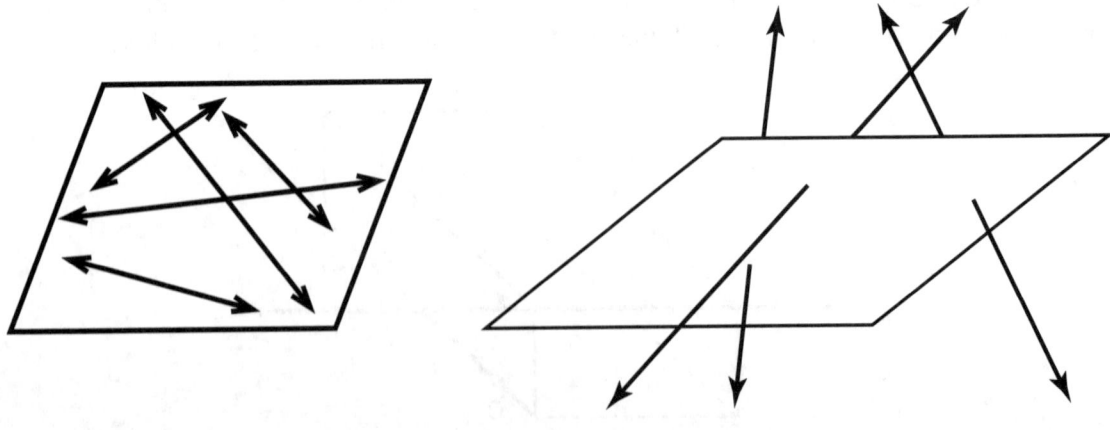

Angle

An **angle** is the set of points in the union of two rays with a common endpoint. Usually, it is stated that these two rays must not belong to the same line. This means that the angles considered in elementary school mathematics are acute, right, and obtuse angles.

In the illustration below, O is the endpoint of $\overrightarrow{OA}$ and O is the endpoint of $\overrightarrow{OB}$. The union of the two rays $\overrightarrow{OA}$ and $\overrightarrow{OB}$ is the angle AOB. Point O is the **vertex** of the angle and $\overrightarrow{OA}$ and $\overrightarrow{OB}$ are **sides**. Angles may be named in several different ways. The angle illustrated may be named ∠AOB or ∠BOA. The symbol "∠" is read "angle." When three letters are used to name an angle, the letter designating the vertex is in the middle.

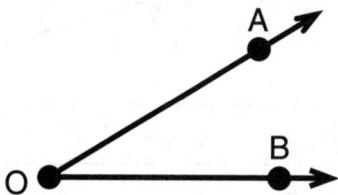

The angle may also be named ∠O. Notice that ∠O is not the same as O, which names a point.

Numerals are also used to name angles. In the illustrations below, the angles are designated as ∠A and ∠1.

An angle has an exterior and an interior. The **interior** is the set of points inside the angle, and the **exterior** is the set of points outside the angle. An angle separates a plane into three sets of points: the set of points in the exterior of the angle, the set of points in the angle, and the set of points in the interior of the angle.

In the following illustration of an angle ABC, the points G and O are in the interior of the angle and the points M, U, and T are in the exterior of the angle. The points A, B, and C are points in the angle.

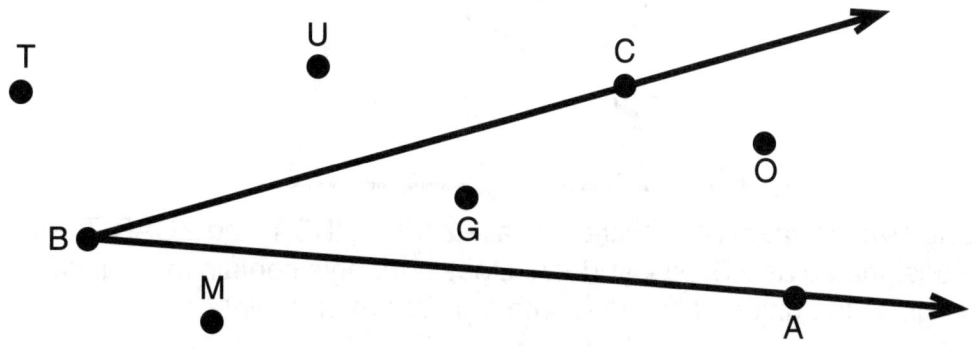

More precisely, the interior of an angle may be described as the intersection of sets of points. Ray BA is on line AB and ray BC is on Line BC. Each line separates the plane into two half planes. The interior of angle ABC is the intersection of the set of points in the half plane on the C side of line AB and the set of points in the half plane on the A side of line BC. The cross hatching in the illustration below represents the intersection of the two sets of points and, therefore, the interior of angle ABC.

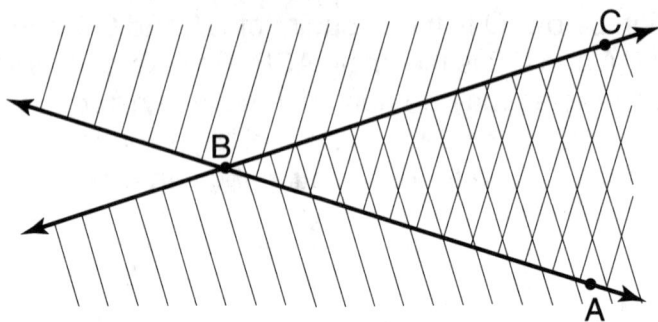

Polygon

A **polygon** is the union of the sets of points in three or more line segments. Each of the following is a polygon.

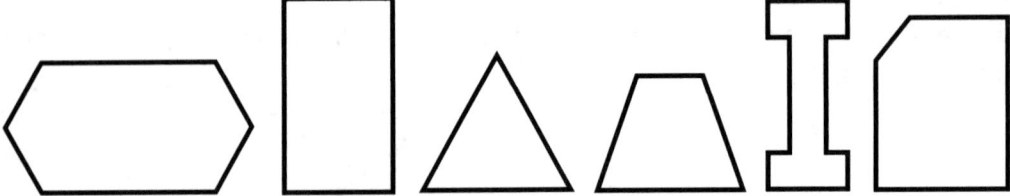

Triangle

The simplest polygon, which is the union of the sets of points in three line segments, is a **triangle**. The triangle represented below is the set of points in $\overline{AB} \cup \overline{BC} \cup \overline{CA}$. The triangle contains these points and only these points. No other points of the plane are in the triangle but are either in the interior or in the exterior of the triangle. $\overline{AB}$, $\overline{BC}$, and $\overline{CA}$ are sides of the triangle. A, B, and C are vertices (plural of vertex).

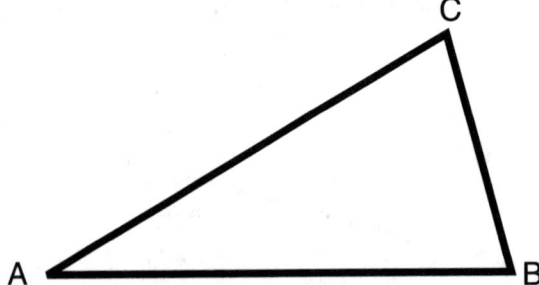

The angles associated with the triangle are ∠ABC, ∠BCA, and ∠CAB. These angles may also be designated as ∠B, ∠C, and ∠A. Does a triangle contain its angles? Remember that an angle is the union of two rays with a common endpoint.

Quadrilateral

A **quadrilateral** is a polygon that is the union of the sets of points in four line segments. Quadrilateral ABCD below is the set of points $\overline{AB} \cup \overline{BC} \cup \overline{CD} \cup \overline{DA}$. The sides of the quadrilateral are $\overline{AB}$, $\overline{BC}$, $\overline{CD}$, and $\overline{DA}$. The vertices of the quadrilateral are A, B, C, and D.

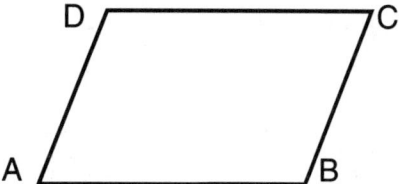

The angles associated with the quadrilateral are ∠ABC, ∠BCD, ∠CDA, and ∠DAB. The angles may also be designated as ∠A, ∠B, ∠C, and ∠D. Does a quadrilateral contain its angles?

A quadrilateral with its opposite sides parallel is a **parallelogram**.

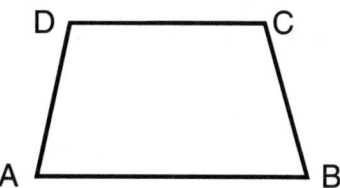

A quadrilateral with one and only one pair of parallel sides is a **trapezoid**.

Other Polygons

A **pentagon** is a polygon that is the union of the sets of points in five line segments. Pentagon ABCDE below is the set of points $\overline{AB} \cup \overline{BC} \cup \overline{CD} \cup \overline{DE} \cup \overline{EA}$.

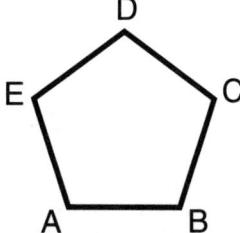

Polygons with more than five sides may be similarly defined. Those with six, seven, eight, nine, and ten sides are known, respectively, as hexagons, heptagons, octagons, nonagons, and decagons.

Basic Geometry   POINTS—LINES—PLANES: Polygonal Regions/Symbols for Geometric Figures

Polygonal Regions

A **polygonal region** is the union of the set of points in a polygon and the set of points in the interior of the polygon. The pictures below represent sets of points called polygonal regions.

   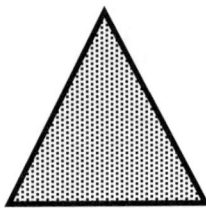

A polygon is a union of line segments and has only length. The region is a surface and has an area.

Symbols for Geometric Figures

Kind of Figure	How Named	How Drawn
1. Segment	$\overline{AB}$	A———B
2. Ray	$\overrightarrow{AB}$	A———B→
3. Line	$\overleftrightarrow{AB}$	←A———B→
4. Angle	∠ABC, ∠B, or ∠1	rays from B to A and B to C

Basic Geometry POINTS—LINES—PLANES: Exercises

Name _____ Date _____

Exercises

1. Draw a line segment PQ. Then draw two other line segments that have Q as an endpoint.

2. Draw a line segment CD. Mark a point O between C and D. Draw a ray OK.

3. Draw an angle TOM. Mark Points C, A, and N inside the angle.

4. Draw a ray HI. Draw a segment HO.

5. ◄—————R●—————A●—————Y●—————►

   a) Three different names for the above line are _____ , _____ , and _____ .

   b) Three different segments on the above line are _____ , _____ , and _____ .

   c) Three different rays on the above line are _____ , _____ , and _____ .

6. Draw lines AB, CD, and EF so that they are concurrent at a point K.

7. Draw a triangle SAM.

Basic Geometry POINTS—LINES—PLANES: Exercises

Name _____ Date _____

8. Draw a quadrilateral JUDY.

9. Draw a pentagon FRANK.

10. Draw a quadrilateral ABCD. Draw a triangle XYZ inside quadrilateral ABCD. Draw a pentagon MNOPQ outside the quadrilateral.

11. Find the following answers.

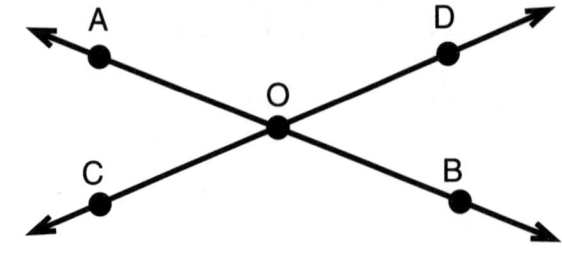

a) $\overleftrightarrow{AB} \cap \overleftrightarrow{CD}$ = _____

b) $\overrightarrow{OA} \cup \overrightarrow{OD}$ = _____

c) $\overrightarrow{OB} \cup \overrightarrow{OA}$ = _____

d) $\overline{OA} \cup \overline{OB}$ = _____

e) $\overrightarrow{OC} \cup \overrightarrow{OA}$ = _____

12.

$\overleftrightarrow{AB}$ and $\overleftrightarrow{CD}$ are parallel lines.

$\overleftrightarrow{AB} \cap \overleftrightarrow{CD}$ = _____

© Mark Twain Media, Inc., Publisher

Basic Geometry POINTS—LINES—PLANES: Discovery Exercise

Name _____ Date _____

Discovery Exercise

1. In the exercises that follow, the dots represent points in a plane. In each exercise, connect the dots in all possible ways by using a ruler. Before you draw the segments for each set of points, count the number of points and try to predict the number of possible segments. Then on the next page, record in the table the actual number of segments you drew.

A

B

C

D

E

F

Basic Geometry   POINTS—LINES—PLANES: Discovery Exercise

Name _____ Date _____

2. After you complete the six exercises on the previous page, you may be able to discover a pattern. Use this pattern to find the number of possible segments when there are eight, nine, or ten points. Fill out the following chart with your findings.

Plane	Number of Points	Number of Segments
A	2	1
B	3	3
C	4	6
D	5	
E	6	
F	7	
	8	
	9	
	10	

3. Can you find a possible relationship between the number of points and the total number of segments?

Let **p** represent the number of points.
Let **s** represent the number of segments.

s = _____

Basic Geometry   CONGRUENCE: Congruence Pre-Test Activities

Name _____ Date _____

CONGRUENCE

Congruence Pre-Test Activities

1. Connect with lines the figures that have the same size and the same shape.

a)

b)

c)

d)

e)

f)

g)

h)

i)

j)

k)

l)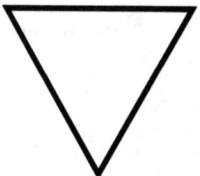

© Mark Twain Media, Inc., Publisher

Basic Geometry CONGRUENCE: Congruence Pre-Test Activities

Name _____ Date _____

2. Connect with lines the figures that have the same size and the same shape.

a)

b)

c)

d)

e)

f)

g)

h)

i)

j)

k)

l)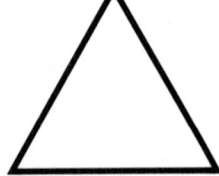

Basic Geometry   CONGRUENCE: Congruence Pre-Test Activities

Name _____ Date _____

3. Trace segment AB on a thin sheet of paper. Then by placing the drawing over each of the other segments, determine which segments are the same length as segment AB. Circle those segments.

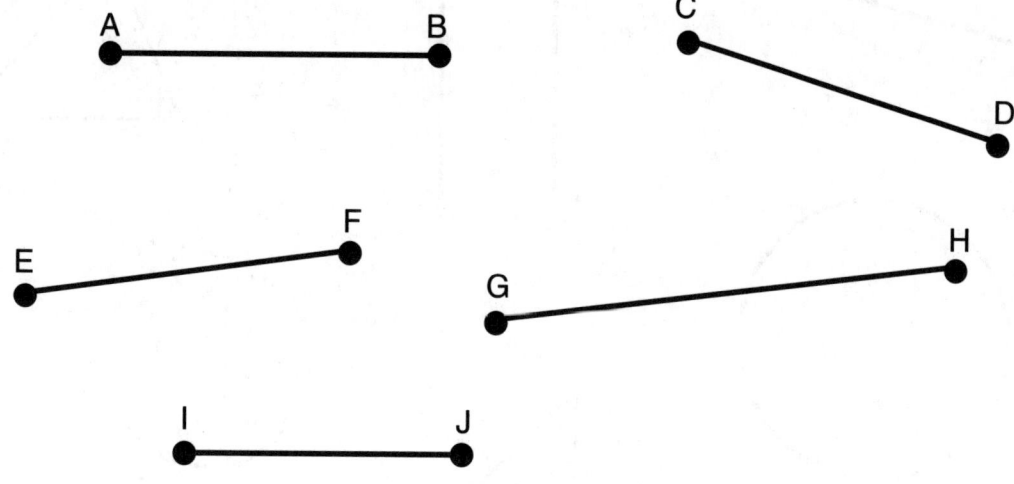

4. Trace angle ABC on a thin sheet of paper. Then by placing the drawing over each of the other angles, determine which angles are the same size as angle ABC. Circle those angles.

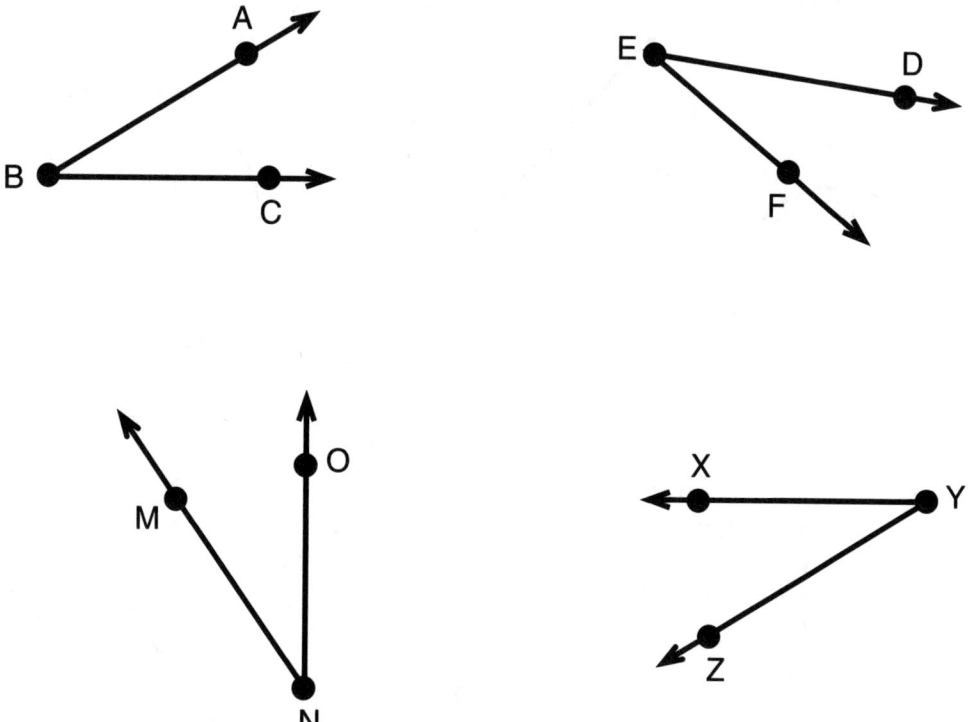

Basic Geometry CONGRUENCE: Congruence Pre-Test Activities

Name _____ Date _____

5. Can you find pairs of figures that look as if a tracing of one of the figures would fit exactly on the other figure? Connect the matching figures with a line.

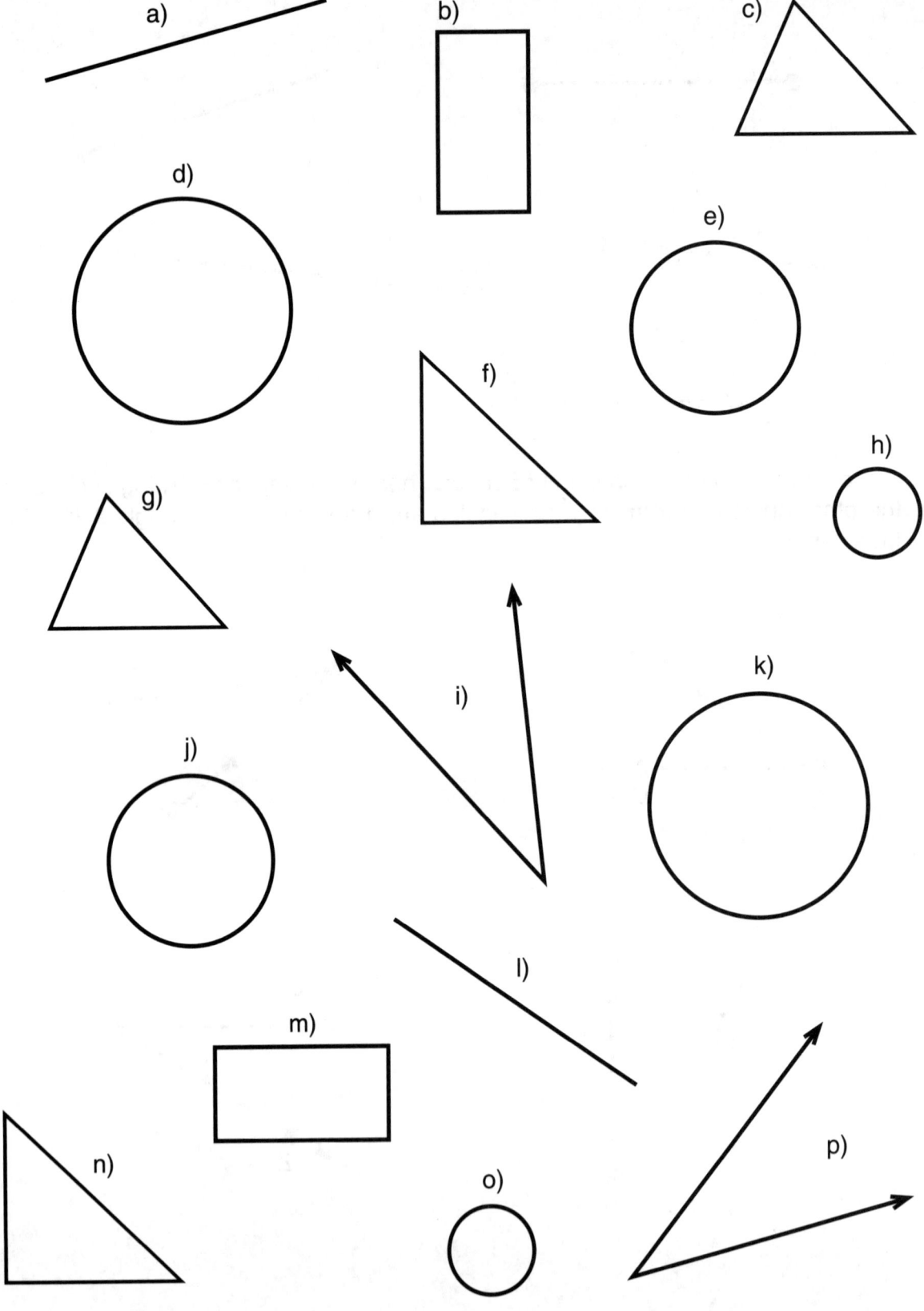

CONGRUENCE

None of the properties of geometric figures described in the preceding chapter depended upon the notion of size. However, the concept of size is basic to the definitions of such familiar figures as right angles, rectangles, squares, equilateral triangles, and so on.

Although geometric figures are abstract ideas, pictures and physical models are used to help develop important properties.

Two line segments, two angles, two closed plane curves, two plane regions, and so on are said to be **congruent** if they are exactly the same shape and size. Below are pictures of pairs of congruent figures.

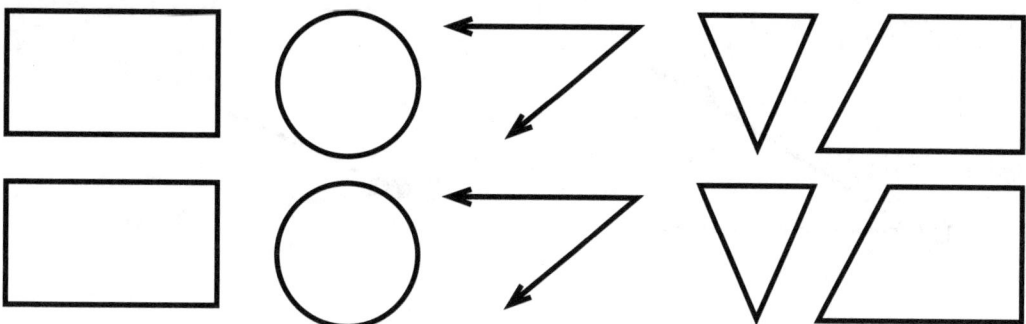

How can you show that the figures in each pair are congruent? Using thin paper, trace the figures in the lower row, and then place the traced figures over the corresponding ones in the upper row. Are the corresponding figures the same size and shape?

Congruence and Equality

In older texts, the word "equals" instead of "congruent" was used to state the relationship between line segments or between angles that had exactly the same size. The word "equals" is now widely accepted in mathematics to mean that two sets contain exactly the same elements or to mean that two numerals are names for the same number. These uses of "equals" are illustrated below.

Equality of sets: If A = {1, 2, 3} and B = {2, 1, 3}, then A = B.
Equality of numbers: 5 + 6 = 4 + 7

The word "congruent" is now used to state the relationship between two geometric figures that have the same size and shape. In the illustration below, $\overline{AB}$ is congruent to $\overline{CD}$.

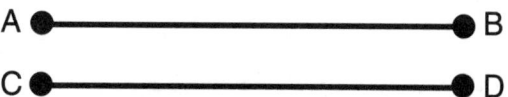

That $\overline{AB}$ is congruent to $\overline{CD}$ is written in symbols, "$\overline{AB} \cong \overline{CD}$." The symbol "$\cong$" is read "is congruent to."

Basic Geometry   CONGRUENCE: Congruent Line Segments/Congruent Angles/Right Angles

Congruent Line Segments

Congruent line segments have the same length. $\overline{AB}$ and $\overline{CD}$ in the preceding illustration are representations of congruent line segments.

If a careful tracing of $\overline{AB}$ is made on thin paper and the tracing placed over $\overline{CD}$ so that A coincides with C, then B may be made to coincide with D.

Congruent Angles

Two angles may be congruent. In the illustration below, ∠ABC is congruent to ∠DEF (∠ABC ≅ ∠DEF).

If a careful tracing of ∠ABC is made on thin paper, and the tracing is placed over ∠DEF so that B and E coincide, the tracing may be rotated so that the corresponding sides of the angles also lie on one another. This illustrates the meaning of the word "congruent" when it is applied to angles. All rays have the same length, regardless of how they are pictured.

Right Angles

When adjacent congruent angles are formed by a ray with an endpoint in a line (or by two lines), as in this diagram, the two angles are called **right angles**.

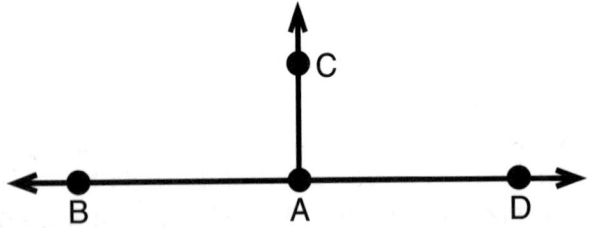

The two right angles in the diagram are ∠BAC and ∠CAD. Also $\overrightarrow{AC}$ is said to be perpendicular to $\overleftrightarrow{BD}$.

Classification of Triangles and Quadrilaterals

The notion of congruence for line segments and angles and the definition of a right angle make it possible to define and classify triangles and quadrilaterals.

1. Triangles
   a) A triangle is **equilateral** if its three sides are congruent.
   b) A triangle is **isosceles** if it has at least two congruent sides.
   c) A triangle is **scalene** if no two of its sides are congruent.

   d) A triangle is **acute** if all of its angles are acute (less than 90 degrees).
   e) A traingle is **obtuse** if it has one obtuse angle (greater than 90 degrees).
   f) A triangle is a **right triangle** if it has one right angle (equal to 90 degrees).

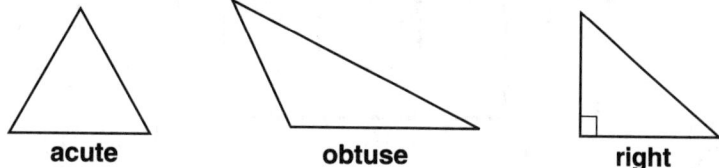

   g) A triangle is **equiangular** if all of its angles have the same measure.

2. Quadrilaterals
   a) A **quadrilateral** is a polygon with four sides.
   b) A **parallelogram** is a quadrilateral with opposite sides parallel.
   c) A **rectangle** is a parallelogram with right angles.
   d) A **square** is a rectangle with adjacent sides congruent.
   e) A **rhombus** is a parallelogram with adjacent sides congruent.
   f) A **trapezoid** is a quadrilateral with only one pair of parallel sides.

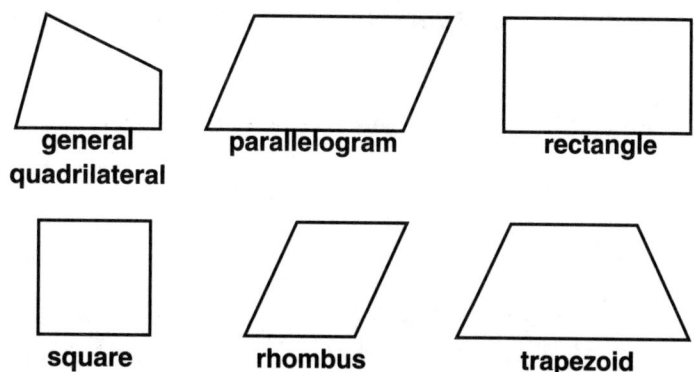

Relationships of Quadrilaterals

The relationships of quadrilaterals may be illustrated by using a Venn diagram. If the universal set is the set of polygons:
1. the set of quadrilaterals is a subset of the set of polygons,
2. the set of parallelograms is a subset of the set of quadrilaterals,
3. the set of rectangles is a subset of the set of parallelograms,
4. the set of squares is a subset of the set of rectangles.

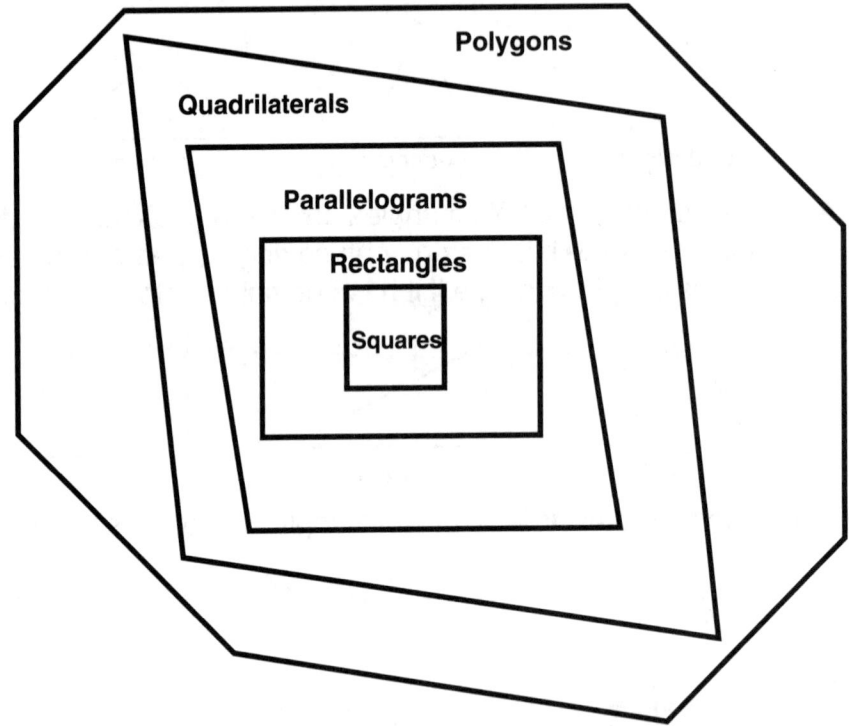

The Venn diagram may be helpful in writing definitions. A definition should name the thing to be defined, should classify it, and should give a distinguishing characteristic. Moreover, a properly stated definition is reversible.

Example: A square is a rectangle with adjacent sides congruent.

This definition may be reversed: A rectangle with adjacent sides congruent is a square.

Basic Geometry — CONGRUENCE: Regular Polygons/Circle

Regular Polygons

A polygon is said to be **regular** if its sides are congruent and its angles are congruent.

A **regular triangle** is an equilateral triangle. The three sides are congruent, and the three angles are congruent.

A **regular quadrilateral** is a square. The four sides are congruent, and the four angles are congruent.

Some regular polygons are illustrated below.

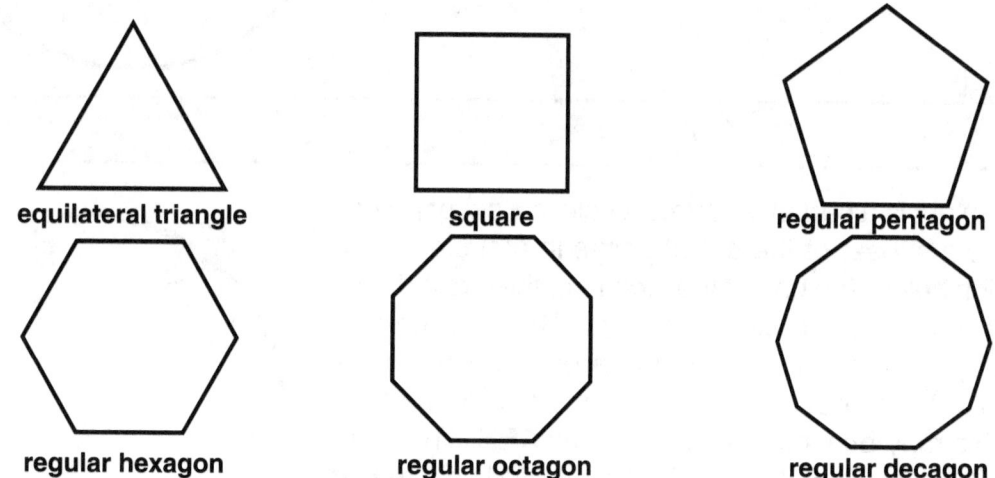

A circle will contain all of the vertices of a regular polygon.

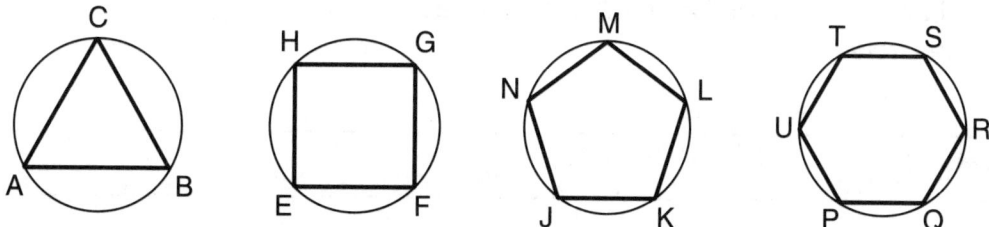

Circle

A **circle** is a closed plane curve with each point in the curve at the same distance from a given interior point called the **center**. The given distance is called the **radius** of the cirlce. The word "radius" may also refer to the segment joining the center with a point on the circle. In the illustration, the center of the circle is O. A and B represent two points on the circle. $\overline{OA}$ and $\overline{OB}$ represent radii (plural of radius) of the circle. All radii of a circle are congruent to one another. The circle illustrated may be designated as "⊙O", which is read "circle O."

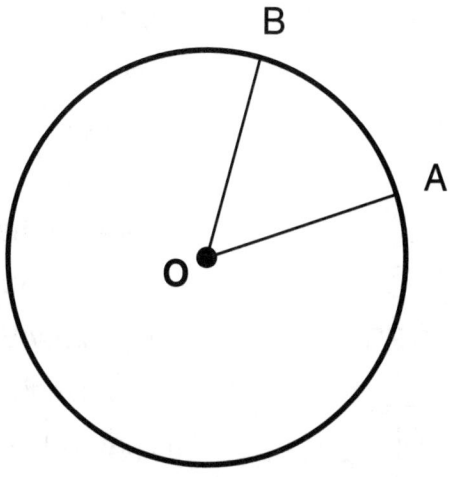

Basic Geometry — CONGRUENCE: Arc/Symbols

A **chord** is a line segment whose endpoints are points on the circle. In the illustration below, $\overline{AB}$ and $\overline{CD}$ represent chords.

A **diameter** is a chord whose endpoints are collinear with the center of a circle. The center is between the endpoints of the diameter. In the illustration, $\overline{CD}$ represents a diameter of the circle. All diameters of a circle are congruent to one another. Arcs CAD and CED are called **semicircles**.

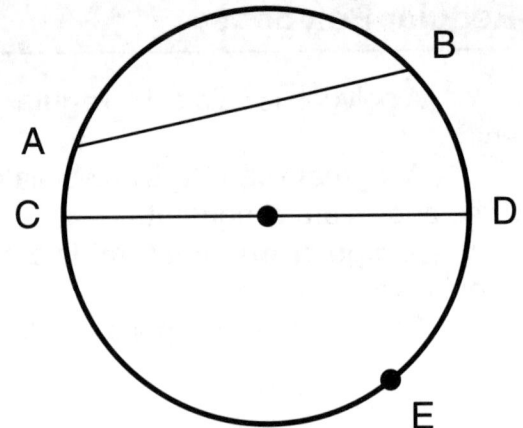

Arc

An arc is a part of a circle. A circle is a set of points; an **arc** is a subset of the set of points in a circle. In the illustration below, the part of the picture of the circle drawn with a heavy line represents an arc. This arc may be named by using its endpoints and a point between the endpoints. In the illustration, the arc may be named arc AEB. This may be written in symbols as $\overset{\frown}{AEB}$. The symbol "$\overset{\frown}{AEB}$" is read "arc AEB." $\overset{\frown}{AEB}$ is classified as a **major arc**. An arc with only the two letters of its endpoints, such as $\overset{\frown}{AB}$, is classified as a **minor arc**. $\overset{\frown}{AB}$ is the heavy-lined area on the circle.

Symbols

Symbol	Meaning
⊙	circle
△	triangle
≅	is congruent to
↔	corresponds to
<	is less than
>	is greater than
$\overset{\frown}{AB}$	minor arc AB or arc AB
$\overset{\frown}{AEB}$	major arc AEB or arc AEB
⊥	is perpendicular to
∥	is parallel to

Basic Geometry   CONGRUENCE: Exercises

Name _____ Date _____

Exercises

1. The dot marked A represents a given point in a plane. Use your ruler to locate 10 different points that are one inch from A.

A •

   a) What kind of pattern do the dots one inch from A seem to make?
   _____

   b) Using A as a center, try to draw a picture of a circle through the points you located.

   c) How was the notion of congruence used in locating these points?
   _____
   _____

2. How is the notion of congruence used in the measurement of length?
   _____
   _____

   a) Find the measure of the long segment below in centimeters. _____

   ____ 1 cm _____

   b) Find the measure of the long segment below in inches. _____

   _____ 1 in. _____

3. How is the notion of congruence used in the measurement of area?
   _____
   _____

Basic Geometry   CONGRUENCE: Exercises

Name _____   Date _____

a) Find the measure of the area of this rectangular region in square centimeters.

_____

1 square cm

4. Examine the figures in each pair to determine whether they are congruent. Write "yes" if they are congruent or "no" if they are not congruent. In some cases you may need to trace one of the figures and fit it over the other one in the pair to determine whether they are the same shape and size.

a) _____   b) _____   c) _____

      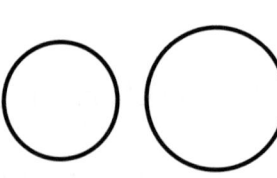

d) _____   e) _____   f) _____

    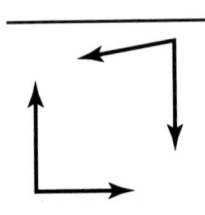

g) _____   h) _____   i) _____

j) _____   k) _____   l) _____   m) _____

© Mark Twain Media, Inc., Publisher

Basic Geometry

CONGRUENCE: Exercises

Name _____ Date _____

5. Draw a scalene right triangle.

6. Is it possible to draw an obtuse right triangle? If not, why?
_____
_____

7. Is an isosceles triangle also an equilateral triangle, or is an equilateral triangle also an isosceles triangle?
_____
_____

8. Measure the angles of an equilateral triangle. How else can you classify an equilateral triangle by the measurement of its angles?
_____
_____

9. Is a square always a rhombus? Is a rhombus always a square?
_____
_____

10. Is a parallelogram always a rectangle? Is a rectangle always a parallelogram?
_____
_____

11. How does a trapezoid differ from a parallelogram?
_____
_____

12. Is it possible for a quadrilateral to be a trapezoid and a parallelogram? Why or why not?
_____
_____

Basic Geometry CONGRUENCE: Exercises

Name _____ Date _____

13. Slash marks and arcs are often used to denote the corresponding parts of congruent figures.

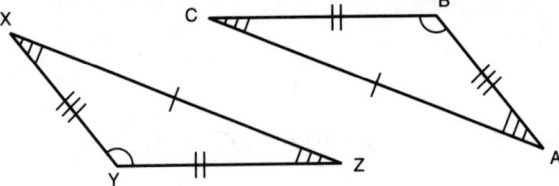

In the above triangles, the following parts correspond:

∠X ↔ ∠A   ∠Y ↔ ∠B   ∠Z ↔ ∠C

$\overline{XY}$ ↔ $\overline{AB}$ $\overline{YZ}$ ↔ $\overline{BC}$ $\overline{ZX}$ ↔ $\overline{CA}$

For any two congruent figures, order the letters representing the vertices so that the correspondence is indicated. In the above illustration, the order of the letters to indicate congruence of the triangles would be as follows.

△XYZ ≅ △ABC

a) For the two congruent triangles below, determine the corresponding angles and the corresponding sides.

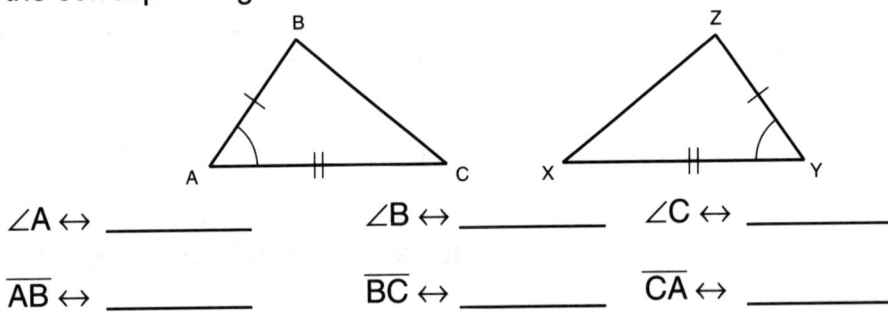

∠A ↔ _____   ∠B ↔ _____   ∠C ↔ _____

$\overline{AB}$ ↔ _____ $\overline{BC}$ ↔ _____ $\overline{CA}$ ↔ _____

Complete the sentence: △ABC ≅ _____

b) Repeat the above exercise with the pair of congruent quadrilaterals given below.

 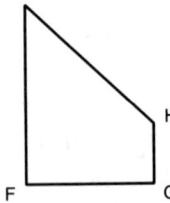

Basic Geometry

CONGRUENCE: Exercises

Name _____ Date _____

14. Sometimes appearances are deceiving. Examine each of the following illustrations and then answer the questions.

   a) Are the vertical segments parallel? _____

   b) Are the two hexagonal shapes in the center of each group congruent? _____

   c) Which segments are congruent? Disregard the arrowheads. _____

   d) Look intently at the following figure for a few seconds. What do you see? _____
   _____

© Mark Twain Media, Inc., Publisher   33

Basic Geometry CONGRUENCE: Exercises

Name _____ Date _____

e) Does the segment on the right belong to the same line as one of the segments on the left? _____

f) What is the shape of figure XYZ? _____

g) Glance at this picture. What do you see? _____

_____

Now look intently at it again. What do you see? _____

_____

h) Are AB and CD line segments or are they curved? _____

Basic Geometry   CONGRUENCE: Visual Aid for Geometry Activity

Name _____ Date _____

Visual Aid for Geometry Activity

To help children understand the linear nature of polygons, a length of cord or heavy string is suggested as a geometry aid. With this, children can fashion triangles, quadrilaterals, pentagons, and so on.

The cord becomes a more valuable tool for measurement and for the representation of the various kinds of triangles, quadrilaterals, and so on, if knots are tied at intervals of one foot.

The linear nature of each figure, and consequently the linear nature of the perimeter, may be illustrated by forming the figure and then showing it as one long segment.

The perimeter of the square may be found in several different ways. A child may simply count the number of feet of cord it takes to make the figure. Another may see that since the length of each side is four feet, he or she can find the measure of the perimeter by addition: 4 + 4 + 4 + 4 = 16. The perimeter is 16 feet. Still another may discover that since the length of each side is 4, he or she can find the measure of the perimeter by multiplication: 4 x 4 = 16. The perimeter is 16 feet. From such observations, children can discover the meaning of the perimeter and can help develop formulas for the measures of the perimeters of various figures.

© Mark Twain Media, Inc., Publisher

Basic Geometry

CONGRUENCE: Area Activity

Name _____ Date _____

Area Activity

The area of a triangle or quadrilateral can be found by knowing the lengths of the base of each figure and the height of each figure.

The area of a triangle is the same regardless of which classification of triangle you are dealing with. The area, **A**, is found by multiplying one-half times the length of the base of the triangle times the height of the triangle.

right triangle   **acute triangle**   **obtuse triangle**

The area of a quadrilateral depends on the particular classification of the quadrilateral. If it is a parallelogram, rectangle, square, or rhombus, the area, **A**, is found by multiplying the length of the base of the quadrilateral times the height of the quadrilateral.

parallelogram   **rectangle**   **square**   **rhombus**

The area of a trapezoid is a little different. The area of a trapezoid depends on the lengths of the parallel sides and the height of the trapezoid (which is the distance between the parallel sides). The area, **A**, of a trapezoid is one-half of the sum of the lengths of the parallel sides (b_1 and b_2) times the height of the trapezoid.

© Mark Twain Media, Inc., Publisher

Basic Geometry CONGRUENCE: Area Activity

Name _____ Date _____

Find the areas of the figures below.

1. _____

   Right triangle with legs 12 and 9.

2. _____

   Rectangle with sides 6 and 8.

3. _____

   Trapezoid with top 5, height 10, bottom 10.

4. _____

   Parallelogram with height 8 and base 12.

5. _____

   Triangle with base 12 and height 3.

6. _____

   Square with side 5.

7. _____

   Figure with measurements 6, 12, and 5.

8. _____

   Triangle with height 9 and base 6.

9. _____

   Rhombus/parallelogram with side 6, height 7, and 6.

© Mark Twain Media, Inc., Publisher

CONVEX AND CONCAVE FIGURES

Convex Figures

The points A and B located below belong to the set of points in the figure. Draw the segment that has A and B as endpoints.

Do any of the points of the segment AB **in** the set of points belong to the figure itself?

Are any of the points of the segment AB **inside** the figure?

Are any of the points of the segment AB **outside** the figure?

Select any two distinct points A and B so that they are members of the set of points in the figure below. Try to select these points so that the segment AB goes outside the figure.

Select other points that are members of the set of points in the figure. Connect pairs of points. Can you find any segment that lies partly outside the figure?

You should find that none of the segments go outside the figure. This is the distinguishing characteristic of a **convex** figure. If a line segment with endpoints in a simple closed figure contains no points in the exterior of the figure, the figure is a convex figure. The following are convex figures.

Basic Geometry — CONVEX AND CONCAVE FIGURES: Concave Figures

Concave Figures

The points A and B located below belong to the set of points in the figure. Draw the segment that has A and B as endpoints.

Are any of the points of the segment AB **in** the set of points in the figure?

Are any of the points of the segment AB **inside** the figure?

Are any of the points of the segment AB **outside** the figure?

Notice that a part of the segment AB is outside the figure. This is a characteristic of a **concave** figure. If two points can be chosen in a simple closed figure so that a line segment with these points as endpoints has points in the exterior of the figure, the figure is a concave figure. The following are concave figures.

Basic Geometry

CONVEX AND CONCAVE FIGURES: Exercises

Name _____ Date _____

Exercises

1. Draw a convex quadrilateral and a concave quadrilateral.

2. Draw a concave hexagon, and then draw a convex pentagon inside it.

3. Draw a convex polygon with seven sides, and then draw a convex hexagon outside it.

4. Draw a concave pentagon inside a convex quadrilateral.

LINES OF SYMMETRY

Fold a piece of paper in halves, cut out a design along the fold, and then open the paper. You will see two congruent shapes, one on each side of the fold.

Fold another piece of paper and then place a drop of paint or colored glue on the inside along the fold. Press the paper firmly together to scatter the paint or glue. Again unfold the paper. Does the fold separate the paint or glue image into two congruent parts?

Line Symmetry

If a line through a plane figure is such that it separates the figure so that the part on one side is an exact reflection of the part on the other side, then the figure has **line symmetry**.

The notion of symmetry for plane figures involves the concepts of congruence and of a reflection, or mirror image. A line of symmetry must separate the figure into two congruent parts.

The figure below shows hexagon ABCDEF. $\overleftrightarrow{AD}$ is a line of symmetry. Trapezoid ABCD is congruent to trapezoid DEFA, and if you hold a mirror vertically along $\overleftrightarrow{AD}$, the part of the hexagon you can see, together with its reflection in the mirror, makes up the whole hexagon.

A line of symmetry not only separates the figure into two congruent parts, but it also separates the figure so that one of the parts can be placed exactly upon the other by reflecting one half of the figure in the line of symmetry. In other words, when you "fold the figure over the line of symmetry" the two halves fit together. If you fold a rectangle that is not a square over a diagonal, will the two triangles fall upon one another? Is the line along the diagonal a line of symmetry in this case?

Basic Geometry	LINES OF SYMMETRY

Name _____ Date _____

Some figures have more than one line of symmetry.

A rectangle that is not a square has two lines of symmetry.

An equilateral triangle has three lines of symmetry.

A circle has an unlimited number of lines of symmetry.

A square has four lines of symmetry.

Some figures have no lines of symmetry.

© Mark Twain Media, Inc., Publisher

Basic Geometry   LINES OF SYMMETRY: Exercises

Name _____ Date _____

Exercises

1. How many lines of symmetry are in each letter of the following word?

GEOMETRY

_____

_____

2. Fold a sheet of copy or typing paper to determine the two lines of symmetry for that sheet of paper.

3. Fold a sheet of copy or typing paper diagonally. Is the diagonal line a line of symmetry?

_____

4. How many lines of symmetry are there in each of these regular polygons?

a) _____   b) _____   c) _____   d) _____   e) _____

5. Draw the lines of symmetry of each of the following figures.

a)

b)

c)

d)

e)

© Mark Twain Media, Inc., Publisher   43

Basic Geometry   MEASUREMENT OF ANGLES

Name _____ Date _____

MEASUREMENT OF ANGLES

Degrees

A basic concept in direct measurement is that the unit of measurement must be of the same nature as the thing to be measured. In the measurement of angles, the unit of measurement is an **angle of one degree**.

The number of degrees in an angle is called its measure. In the illustration above, the measure of angle AOB is 10. There are 10° in ∠AOB. The symbol for measure of an angle (in degrees), such as angle AOB, is "m ∠AOB = n" where "n" is a number representing the measure of the angle. The symbol "m ∠AOB" is read "the measure of angle AOB."

1. Use the illustration above to find the measures of the following angles.

   a) m ∠AOC _____

   b) m ∠AOD _____

   c) m ∠AOE _____

   d) m ∠AOF _____

   e) m ∠BOC _____

   f) m ∠COF _____

Basic Geometry   MEASUREMENT OF ANGLES

Name _____ Date _____

An angle may be measured with a protractor. Some protractors are marked in degrees with one scale that is read clockwise and another scale that is read counterclockwise. The sketch below shows a semicircular protractor placed on a set of rays with a common endpoint "O". The base of the protractor is placed evenly on the line segment AH.

2. Find the measure in degrees of each angle designated below.

a) m ∠AOB = _____

b) m ∠AOE = _____

c) m ∠GOH = _____

d) m ∠FOA = _____

e) m ∠DOA = _____

f) m ∠COA = _____

g) m ∠COD = _____
   Move a protractor so that the zero
   ray lies along $\vec{OC}$ (or $\vec{OD}$)

h) m ∠FOG = _____
   Move a protractor so that the zero
   ray lies along $\vec{OG}$ (or $\vec{OF}$)

i) m ∠COB = _____

j) m ∠DOG = _____

k) m ∠HOB = _____

© Mark Twain Media, Inc., Publisher

Basic Geometry MEASUREMENT OF ANGLES: Special Names for Angles According to Their Measures

Name _____   Date _____

Special Names for Angles According to Their Measures

An **acute angle** is an angle whose measure in degrees is less than 90. Verify by measuring each angle below that it is an acute angle.

A **right angle** is an angle whose measure in degrees is 90. Verify by measurement that the following represent right angles.

An **obtuse angle** is an angle whose measure in degrees is greater than 90 but less than 180. Verify by measurement that the following represent obtuse angles.

Complementary and Supplementary Angles

Two angles are considered **complementary angles** if the sum of their angles is exactly 90 degrees. Two angles are considered **supplementary angles** if the sum of their angles is 180 degrees.

3. Which angles in the above diagram are complementary? _____

_____

4. Which angles in the above diagram are supplementary? _____

Basic Geometry
MEASUREMENT OF ANGLES: Exercises

Name _____ Date _____

Exercises

1. Classify the following triangles:

   a) according to relative lengths of sides.

   [Triangle with sides 3, 5, 7]   [Triangle with sides 8, 3, 8]   [Triangle with sides 5, 5, 5]

   _____   _____   _____

   b) according to the measures of the angles.

   [Triangle with angles 110°, 40°, 30°]   [Triangle with angles 70°, 40°, 70°]   [Triangle with angles 90°, 30°, 60°]

   _____   _____   _____

2. Several experiments may be used to help students discover that the sum of the measures of the angles of a plane triangle is the same for all triangles. Basic to this discovery is the knowledge of the sum of the measures in degrees of three angles such as those illustrated in the diagram below.

   a) $\overleftrightarrow{AB}$ is a straight line with P some point on $\overleftrightarrow{AB}$. Angles 1, 2, and 3 have the same vertex P. Use a protractor to measure the three angles.

   The sum of the measures of the three angles is _____ .

   b) Draw a triangle and cut it out. Then draw a line and select some point P on the line. Tear off the three vertices and arrange them as illustrated with the vertices at P.

   What does this seem to demonstrate about the sum of the measures of the three angles of a triangle?

   _____

   _____

© Mark Twain Media, Inc., Publisher

Basic Geometry MEASUREMENT OF ANGLES: Exercises

Name _____ Date _____

c) Draw a triangle ABC and cut it out.

Find the midpoint of $\overline{AC}$ and the midpoint of $\overline{BC}$. Draw the midsegment and fold the triangular region over the midsegment so that C falls on $\overline{AB}$. Fold again so that angles 1, 2, and 3 are in the position shown below.

What does this seem to demonstrate about the sum of the measures of the three angles?

_____

d) Use a protractor to measure each angle of the triangles pictured below. Record the measures in the table and find the sum of the measures for each triangle.

Angle	Triangle I	Triangle II	Triangle III	Triangle IV
∠A				
∠B				
∠C				
Sum				

What does the sum of the measures of the three angles for each triangle appear to be? _____

Now find the average of the four sums. The average is _____.

Basic Geometry   MEASUREMENT OF ANGLES: Exercises

Name _____ Date _____

e) △ABC is a triangle with a line XY through vertex C and parallel to base AB.

1) What do you know about the sum of the measures in degrees of ∠1, ∠2, and ∠3?

   _____

2) Using your protractor, find the following measures.

   m ∠A = _____   m ∠B = _____

   m ∠1 = _____   m ∠3 = _____

3) How do the measures of ∠A and ∠1 compare? _____

4) How do the measures of ∠B and ∠3 compare? _____

5) How does the sum of the measures of ∠1, ∠2, and ∠3 compare with the sum of the measures of ∠A, ∠B, and ∠2?

   _____

3. △ABC is an equilateral triangle. The three sides of an equilateral triangle are congruent. Measure each angle and record the information.

   a) m ∠A = _____

   b) m ∠B = _____

   c) m ∠C = _____

   d) What can you conclude about the three angles of an equilateral triangle?

   _____

   _____

Basic Geometry   MEASUREMENT OF ANGLES: Exercises

Name _____   Date _____

4. △ABC is an isosceles triangle. An isosceles triangle has at least two congruent sides. $\overline{AC}$ is congruent to $\overline{BC}$. Measure each angle and record the information.

   a) m ∠A = _____

   b) m ∠B = _____

   c) m ∠C = _____

   d) What can you conclude about ∠A and ∠B?
   _____

5. △ABC is a scalene triangle. A scalene triangle has no congruent sides. Measure the sides and angles and record the information below.

   a) longest side _____

   b) next largest side _____

   c) shortest side _____

   d) largest angle _____

   e) next largest angle _____

   f) smallest angle _____

   g) What conclusions can you draw from this exercise?
   _____
   _____

© Mark Twain Media, Inc., Publisher

Basic Geometry — MEASUREMENT OF ANGLES: Exercises

Name _____ Date _____

6. The sum of the measures in degrees of the three angles of a triangle is 180. This information can be used to determine the sum of the measures of the angles of a polygon with any number of sides (without measurement). For each polygon that follows, draw all possible diagonals from vertex A. Assume all polygons to be regular (all sides with the same length and all angles congruent).

Complete the following table.

Number of sides	Number of angles	Number of diagonals	Number of triangles	Angle Sum of one triangle	Angle Sum of the polygon	Measure of each angle
3	3	0	1	180	180	60
4	4	1	2	180	360	90
5	5					
6						
7						
8						
9						
10						
11						
12						
n						

a) State a relationship between the number of sides of any polygon and the number of diagonals that can be drawn from one vertex.

_____

b) State a relationship between the number of sides of a polygon and the number of triangles formed by the sides and by the diagonals from one vertex.

_____

c) What is the sum of the measures of the three angles of one triangle?

_____

d) What is the sum of the measures of the interior angles of a polygon of "n" sides?

_____

Basic Geometry MEASUREMENT OF ANGLES: Exercises

Name _____ Date _____

7. $\overleftrightarrow{AB}$ and $\overleftrightarrow{CD}$ are a pair of parallel lines. $\overleftrightarrow{EF}$ is a line that intersects each of the parallel lines. $\overleftrightarrow{EF}$ is called a **transversal**.

Use a protractor to measure each angle in the diagram above. Record the measures in the blanks below.

a) m ∠1 = _____

b) m ∠2 = _____

c) m ∠3 = _____

d) m ∠4 = _____

e) m ∠5 = _____

f) m ∠6 = _____

g) m ∠7 = _____

h) m ∠8 = _____

i) Are angles with the same measure in degrees congruent?

_____, _____, _____, and _____ are congruent angles.

_____, _____, _____, and _____ are congruent angles.

j) Use a color code to show the sets of congruent angles in the picture.

k) What is the sum of the measures of angles 2 and 6? _____

l) What is the sum of the measures of angles 3 and 7? _____

m) What tentative conclusions can you draw about the sum of the measures of two interior angles on the same side of the transversal?

_____

© Mark Twain Media, Inc., Publisher

Basic Geometry MEASUREMENT OF ANGLES: Exercises

Name _____ Date _____

9. In the illustration below, line AB is parallel to line CD. Also, line EF is perpendicular to line CD.

a) What is the measure in degrees of each of the eight angles? _____

b) Is line EF also perpendicular to line AB? _____

c) If a line is perpendicular to one of two parallel lines, is it perpendicular to both of the parallel lines?

_____

d) Are two lines parallel if they are both perpendicular to the same line?

_____

When two parallel lines are cut by a transversal, eight angles are formed. Special names are given to these angles for convenience in discussing them.

Interior angles: 2, 3, 6, and 7

Exterior angles: 1, 4, 5, and 8

Alternate interior angles: 2 and 3, 6 and 7

Alternate exterior angles: 5 and 8, 1 and 4

Corresponding angles: 1 and 3, 5 and 7, 2 and 4, 6 and 8

© Mark Twain Media, Inc., Publisher

Basic Geometry MEASUREMENT OF ANGLES: Exercises

Name _____ Date _____

10. Four angles are associated with a pair of intersecting lines. In the illustration below, angles 1 and 2 are referred to as a pair of vertical angles, and angles 3 and 4 are referred to as a pair of vertical angles.

Use a protractor to measure each angle and record the information in the appropriate blanks.

a) m ∠1 = _____   b) m ∠2 = _____   c) m ∠3 = _____   d) m ∠4 = _____

e) What appears to be true of a pair of vertical angles? _____
_____

11. In the figure below, angle 1 is referred to as an exterior angle of the triangle. Angles A and B are referred to as the two nonadjacent interior angles with reference to exterior angle 1. How are angles A and B related to angle 1?

Find the measure of each of the following angles.

a) m ∠A = _____   b) m ∠B = _____   c) m ∠1 = _____

The measure in degrees of an exterior angle of a triangle is equal to the sum of the measures of the two nonadjacent interior angles.

© Mark Twain Media, Inc., Publisher   54

Basic Geometry   MEASUREMENT OF ANGLES: Exercises

Name _____ Date _____

12. For each of the following figures, the number of degrees in one or more of the angles is given. Without measuring, find the number of degrees in each of the other angles. Write the degrees of each angle on the diagrams.

a)

147°

b)

134°

c)

50°   65°

Basic Geometry • CONSTRUCTIONS

Name _____ Date _____

CONSTRUCTIONS

Since the days of the ancient Greek philosopher, Plato (380 B.C.), a clear distinction has been made between a drawing and a **construction**. Geometry, as practiced by the ancient Greeks, was much like a game, and to play the game, the players followed certain rules. One set of rules concerned the drawing instruments permitted in making constructions.

In a construction, points and lines were determined by using only two instruments, a straightedge (with no marking of any kind on it) and a compass.

The construction depended upon three assumptions:
1) two points determine a straight line.
2) all radii of the same circle are congruent.
3) radii of congruent circles are congruent.

In constructions, points are determined by the intersection of two circles, of two lines, or of a line and a circle. If two congruent circles intersect in two points, each of the points of intersection is the same distance from the centers of the two circles.

In the illustration below, circles A and B are congruent. They intersect in points C and D, each of which is the same distance from points A and B.

Why are $\overline{AC}$, $\overline{AD}$, $\overline{BC}$, and $\overline{BD}$ congruent? _____

_____

In the preceding illustration, the points C and D could have been located at equal distances from A and B by using intersecting arcs of congruent circles. The use of arcs to locate C and D is shown below. $\overline{AC}$, $\overline{AD}$, $\overline{BC}$, and $\overline{BD}$ are congruent segments because they are radii of congruent circles.

By making constructions to represent geometric ideas and by using measurements, students may be able to make many interesting discoveries in Euclidean geometry.

Basic Geometry   CONSTRUCTIONS: Intersection Exercises

Name _____ Date _____

Intersection Exercises

1. In each of the following illustrations, label the point or points of intersection.

a)   b)   c)

d)   e)   f)

g)   h)

i)   j)   k)

2. Draw each segment determined by the two points of intersection of the circles.

a)   b)   c)

Basic Geometry CONSTRUCTIONS: Construct a Line Segment/Bisect a Line Segment

Name _____ Date _____

A. Construct a Line Segment Congruent to a Given Segment

1. Let $\overline{AB}$ be the given segment.
2. Draw any ray PX.
3. With $\overline{AB}$ as radius and with P as center, draw an arc that intersects $\overrightarrow{PX}$ at Q.
4. $\overline{AB} \cong \overline{PQ}$.

Exercise

1. Use a compass to construct a segment that is three times the length of the segment RS.

   R———S

B. Bisect a Line Segment

AB is a line segment. To bisect segment AB is to find its midpoint so that segment AB is divided into two congruent parts.

1. With A as center and a radius greater than one-half $\overline{AB}$, draw arcs above and below $\overline{AB}$.
2. With B as center and with the same radius, draw arcs intersecting the first arcs drawn. Label the points of intersection of the arcs C and D.
3. Draw a straight mark through C and D.
4. Use E to label the point where $\overleftrightarrow{CD}$ intersect $\overline{AB}$.
5. E is the midpoint of $\overline{AB}$.
6. Also, line CD is perpendicular to segment AB, therefore $\overleftrightarrow{CD}$ is the perpendicular bisector of $\overline{AB}$.

Basic Geometry CONSTRUCTIONS: Bisect a Line Segment

Name _____ Date _____

Exercises

1. Measure $\overline{AE}$ and $\overline{EB}$ on the diagram in B on page 58. Are they the same length? ___

2. Select some other point K on $\overline{CD}$. Measure the distance from K to A and from K to B.

   a) How do these distances compare? _____

   b) Do you think that any point on $\overleftrightarrow{CD}$ is the same distance from A and B? _____

3. Use the corner of an index card to determine whether the four angles with vertex E are right angles.

4. Construct the perpendicular bisector of each of the following line segments.

   a)

   b)

5. Below are two triangles. Carefully construct the perpendicular bisector of each side of each triangle.

   a)

   b)

   c) Did the perpendicular bisectors of the sides of triangle ABC meet in the same point? _____

   d) Did the perpendicular bisectors of the sides of triangle DEF meet in the same point? _____

   e) Try to draw a circle that passes through the three vertices of one of the triangles.

The three perpendicular bisectors of the sides of a triangle meet in the same point, that is, they are concurrent. **Concurrent** lines are lines that have a point in common. In the completed diagram that follows, the perpendicular bisectors of the sides of the triangle meet at point O.

© Mark Twain Media, Inc., Publisher

Basic Geometry CONSTRUCTIONS: Construct a Ray

Name _____ Date _____

The point O is the same distance from the vertices A, B, and C. A circle with O as a center and $\overline{OA}$ as a radius will contain the points A, B, and C. The circle O is **circumscribed** about the triangle ABC. The point O is the **circumcenter** of the triangle ABC. The triangle ABC is **inscribed** in circle O because its three vertices belong to the set of points in the circle.

C. Construct a Ray Perpendicular to a Line at a Given Point in the Line.

$\overleftrightarrow{AB}$ is a line with P a point in the line. A ray is to be constructed so that it is perpendicular to $\overleftrightarrow{AB}$ at P.

1. Using your compass, use P as the center and mark points C and D on $\overleftrightarrow{AB}$ so that $\overline{PC} \cong \overline{PD}$.
2. With C as center and with a radius greater than $\overline{PC}$, draw an arc in the half plane on one side of $\overleftrightarrow{AB}$.
3. With D as center and with the same radius, draw an arc that intersects the arc with center C.
4. Label E the point of intersection of the arcs.
5. Draw $\overrightarrow{PE}$.
6. $\overrightarrow{PE}$ is perpendicular to $\overleftrightarrow{AB}$.

Exercises

1. Use the corner of an index card to test the two angles at P to determine whether they are right angles.

Basic Geometry   CONSTRUCTIONS: Construct a Perpendicular

Name _____ Date _____

2. Below are two line segments. Construct a perpendicular at each point labeled P.

a)

b)

3. Construct perpendiculars to segment AB at the points A and B.

D. Construct a Perpendicular From a Point to a Line

$\overleftrightarrow{AB}$ is a line and P is a point not in $\overleftrightarrow{AB}$. Construct a perpendicular from P to $\overleftrightarrow{AB}$.

1. With P as center, draw an arc that intersects $\overleftrightarrow{AB}$ in two points.
2. Label these points C and D.
3. With C as center and with a radius greater than one-half $\overline{CD}$, draw an arc in the half plane not containing P.
4. With D as center and with the same radius, draw an arc that intersects the arc with C as center.
5. Label E the point where the two arcs intersect.
6. Draw $\overrightarrow{PE}$.
7. $\overleftrightarrow{PE}$ is perpendicular to $\overleftrightarrow{AB}$.

Exercises

1. Use the corner of an index card to test the four angles at vertex K to determine whether they are right angles.

Basic Geometry   CONSTRUCTIONS: Construct a Perpendicular

Name _____ Date _____

2. $\overleftrightarrow{AB}$ and $\overleftrightarrow{CD}$ are two different lines. P is a point not in either line. From P construct a perpendicular to each of the lines.

The distance from a given point P to a line is the length of the segment that is perpendicular to the line and that has P as one endpoint and a point in the line as the other endpoint. In the exercise above, the segments from P to $\overleftrightarrow{AB}$ and $\overleftrightarrow{CD}$ were constructed. The distance from P to each of the lines is measured along the perpendicular segment.

3. Construct a perpendicular from M to line XY. In this case, first extend the line to the left of point X.

The length of each **altitude** of a triangle is a distance from a point to a line. For triangle ABC that follows, the three altitudes are shown. The length of segment $\overline{CD}$ is the distance from C to $\overleftrightarrow{AB}$, and $\overline{CD}$ is the altitude to base $\overleftrightarrow{AB}$ of the triangle. Likewise, $\overline{BF}$ is the altitude to base $\overleftrightarrow{AC}$, and $\overline{AE}$ is the altitude to base $\overleftrightarrow{BC}$. Every triangle has three altitudes. The three altitudes of a triangle are concurrent.

© Mark Twain Media, Inc., Publisher

Basic Geometry   CONSTRUCTIONS: Construct a Perpendicular/Bisect a Given Angle

Name _____ Date _____

4. Carefully construct the three altitudes of each of the following triangles.

   a) This is an acute triangle. Are the three altitudes concurrent; that is, do they all meet at the same point?

   _____

   If so, was the point of concurrency inside, in, or outside the triangle?

   _____

   b) This is a right triangle. Were the three altitudes concurrent?

   _____

   Did you need to construct all three altitudes?

   _____

   c) This is an obtuse triangle. Are the three altitudes concurrent?

   _____

   If so, where is the point of concurrency?

   _____

E. Bisect a Given Angle

To bisect the angle ABC means to locate a ray BF so that angle ABF is congruent to angle CBF.

1. Use B as center, and with a convenient radius, draw arcs that intersect rays BA and BC.
2. Label the points of intersection D and E.
3. With a convenient radius, and with D as center, draw an arc in the interior of angle ABC.
4. With the same radius, and with E as center, draw an arc that intersects the arc with center D.
5. Label the point of intersection F.
6. Draw ray BF.
7. Ray BF is the bisector of angle ABC.

© Mark Twain Media, Inc., Publisher

Basic Geometry CONSTRUCTIONS: Bisect a Given Angle

Name _____ Date _____

Exercises

1. Construct the bisector of each of the angles below.

    a)

    b)

2. Below are two triangles. For each triangle, construct the three angle bisectors.

    a)

    b)

The three angle bisectors meet at a point called the **incenter** of the triangle. The point O is the same distance from each side of the triangle.

With O as center and with a radius equal to the distance from O to $\overline{AB}$, a circle may be drawn that contains one point in each side of the triangle. The circle is said to be **inscribed** in the triangle. The triangle is said to be **circumscribed** about the circle.

Basic Geometry   CONSTRUCTIONS: Construct an Angle Congruent to a Given Angle

Name _____ Date _____

F. Construct an Angle Congruent to a Given Angle

Construct an angle congruent to ABC.

1. Use some ray EF as a side of the angle to be contructed and use E for the vertex.
2. With B as center and with some convenient radius, draw an arc that intersects the sides of angle ABC at G and H.
3. With E as center and with the same radius draw an arc that intersects $\overline{EF}$ at K.
4. Using K as center and $\overline{GH}$ as radius, draw an arc that intersects at M the arc whose center is E.
5. Draw $\overrightarrow{EM}$.
6. Angle MEK is congruent to angle ABC.
7. Trace angle ABC on thin paper. Then place the drawing over angle MEK to see if the two angles are the same size.

Exercise

1. Below are two angles. Construct an angle congruent to each.

   a)

   b)

© Mark Twain Media, Inc., Publisher

Basic Geometry   CONSTRUCTIONS: Construct a Triangle Congruent to a Given Triangle/Parallel Line

Name _____ Date _____

G. Construct a Triangle Congruent to a Given Triangle

1. Draw any ray A^1X.
2. Use your compass to measure $\overline{AB}$.
3. With A^1 as one endpoint mark a point on $\overrightarrow{A^1X}$ so that $\overline{A^1B^1} \cong \overline{AB}$.
4. With $\overline{AC}$ as a radius and A^1 as center, draw an arc above $\overline{A^1B^1}$.
5. With $\overline{BC}$ as radius and B^1 as center, draw an arc that intersects the first arc.
6. Label C^1 the point where the arcs intersect.
7. Draw $\overline{A^1C^1}$ and $\overline{B^1C^1}$.
8. Triangles ABC and $A^1B^1C^1$ are congruent.

Exercise

1. Construct a triangle congruent to the given triangle.

H. Construct a Line Through a Given Point and Parallel to a Given Line

Through P construct a line parallel to $\overleftrightarrow{AB}$.

1. Through P draw any line that intersects $\overleftrightarrow{AB}$ at some point C.
2. With P as a vertex and with $\overrightarrow{CP}$ as one side, construct an angle EPD congruent to angle ACP.
3. The line DP is the required line.

One of the assumptions in Euclidean geometry is that a given point not in a given line is in one and only one line parallel to the given line. This was Euclid's famous **Fifth Postulate**, which is historically significant.

© Mark Twain Media, Inc., Publisher

Basic Geometry   CONSTRUCTIONS: Construct a Line Parallel to a Given Line

Name _____ Date _____

I. Construct a Line Parallel to a Given Line and at a Given Distance From It

$\overleftrightarrow{AB}$ is the given line and **d** is the segment representing the distance between $\overleftrightarrow{AB}$ and the line parallel to $\overleftrightarrow{AB}$.

1. At two points M and N on $\overleftrightarrow{AB}$, construct perpendiculars $\overrightarrow{MR}$ and $\overrightarrow{NS}$.
2. With M as one endpoint, lay off on ray MR a segment MC congruent to **d**.
3. With N as one endpoint, lay off on ray NS a segment ND congruent to **d**.
4. Draw $\overleftrightarrow{CD}$.
5. $\overleftrightarrow{CD}$ is the required line.

The distance between two parallel lines is the length of a segment with an endpoint in each line and perpendicular to the lines.

In the picture, **n** and **m** represent parallel lines. $\overline{AB}$ has one endpoint in **n** and one endpoint in **m**. $\overline{AB}$ is perpendicular to both lines. The length of $\overline{AB}$ is the distance between **n** and **m**.

The altitude of a parallelogram is an example of a distance between parallel lines.

In the illustration, $\overline{EF}$ is called the altitude to either $\overline{AB}$ or $\overline{DC}$. $\overline{GH}$ is called the altitude to either $\overline{AD}$ or $\overline{BC}$.

© Mark Twain Media, Inc., Publisher

Basic Geometry CONSTRUCTIONS: Construct a Line Parallel to a Given Line

Name _____ Date _____

Exercise

You are an engineer responsible for designing the layout of a new city. The city will be located next to a river that runs north-northeast. The southern boundary of the city will be the highway running east to west. Main Street will be the road that runs north to south.

Your job is to map out seven city streets parallel to the highway, five city streets parallel to Main Street, and two city streets parallel to the river. Of the five city streets parallel to Main Street, three must be on the west side of Main Street and two on the east side of Main Street. The only tools you may use are a straight edge and a compass.

Use a protractor for the following questions.

1. What is the measure of each angle in the intersection of the river with the highway?

_____

2. What is the measure of each angle in the intersection of Main Street with the highway?

_____

3. Write the measure of each angle in the intersection of the two streets parallel with the river and their intersections with the highway.

_____

4. At some point the streets parallel to Main Street will intersect the streets parallel to the river. What are the measures of the angles at these intersections?

_____

Basic Geometry CONSTRUCTIONS: Separate a Circle Into Six Congruent Arcs

Name _____ Date _____

J. Separate a Circle Into Six Congruent Arcs

1. Draw a circle with any convenient radius.
2. Using the same radius and any point A in the circle as center, draw an arc that intersects the circle at B.
3. Using the same radius and B as center, draw an arc that intersects the circle at C.
4. Continue this procedure until you have separated the circle into six consecutive arcs.

This particular construction is at the basis of many designs. Connecting consecutive points makes a regular hexagon. It is possible to bisect the arcs and to connect consecutive points to make a regular dodecagon (12-sided polygon).

The following designs are based upon this construction.

Exercise

1. Use this space to make a design of your own.

Basic Geometry   CONSTRUCTIONS: Constructions Exercises

Name _____   Date _____

Constructions Exercises

1. Using $\overline{AB}$ as one side, construct a triangle with each of the sides congruent to $\overline{AB}$. If three sides of a triangle are congruent, the triangle is a(n) _____ triangle.

   A _____ B

2. Using $\overline{AB}$ as one side and $\overline{AC}$ as one of two congruent sides, construct a triangle ABC. If at least two sides of a triangle are congruent, the triangle is a(n) _____ triangle.

   A _____ B

   A _____ C

© Mark Twain Media, Inc., Publisher

Basic Geometry CONSTRUCTIONS: Constructions Exercises

Name _____ Date _____

3. Using your ruler and compass, carefully construct four triangles, each with sides congruent to these three given segments.

     _____ a

     _____ b

     _____ c

Trace one triangle and place the tracing over each of the other three triangles.

a) Can you match the sides and angles? _____

b) Are the triangles the same size? _____

c) What conclusion can you draw? _____

_____

_____

Basic Geometry CONSTRUCTIONS: Constructions Exercises

Name _____ Date _____

4. Using your ruler and compass, carefully construct four triangles, each with two sides congruent to $\overline{AB}$ and $\overline{AC}$ and one angle congruent to angle A. The letters will tell you how the angle is related to the two given sides.

A ——————— B

A ——————————— C

A (angle)

Trace one triangle and place the tracing over each of the other three triangles.

a) Can you match the sides and angles? _____

b) Are the triangles the same size? _____

c) What conclusion can you draw? _____

_____

_____

_____

Basic Geometry

CONSTRUCTIONS: Constructions Exercises

Name _____ Date _____

5. Using your ruler and compass, carefully construct four triangles, each with a side congruent to $\overline{AB}$ and with two angles congruent to the angles A and B. The letters will tell you how the angles are related to the given side.

Trace one triangle and place the tracing over each of the other three triangles.

a) Can you match the sides and angles? _____

b) Are the triangles the same size? _____

c) What conclusion can you draw? _____

_____

_____

© Mark Twain Media, Inc., Publisher

Basic Geometry

CONSTRUCTIONS: Constructions Exercises

Name _____ Date _____

6. Construct a square ABCD with sides congruent to the given segment AB.

A ―――――――――― B

7. Use the given line segments to construct a rectangle ABCD.

―――――――
―――――――――

8. Use a compass to find the measure in inches of each of the segments below.

   1 inch: ―――

a) ―――――――――――――――――
b) ―――――――
c) ――――――――――――――――――――

9. Use a compass to find the measure in centimeters of each of the segments below.

   1 centimeter: ――

a) ―――――――――――――――
b) ――――――――――
c) ―――――――――――――

Basic Geometry CONSTRUCTIONS: Constructions Exercises

Name _____ Date _____

10. There are 10 centimeters in a decimeter. Use a compass to construct a segment that is one decimeter long.

11. Construct a segment that is four centimeters long. Then use this segment to construct an equilateral triangle with sides four centimeters long.

12. In the space below, complete the following steps.

   a) Draw a circle with a diameter of three inches.
   b) Draw a diameter and label the endpoints A and B.
   c) Label some other point C on the circle.
   d) Draw segment AC and BC.
   e) Measure angle ACB.

   f) What seems to be true of angle ACB? _____

Triangle ACB is a triangle **inscribed** in a semicircle, and thus angle ACB is an angle inscribed in a semicircle. An angle inscribed in a semicircle is a right angle.

Basic Geometry CONSTRUCTIONS: Constructions Exercises

Name _____ Date _____

13. A, B, and C are any three distinct points on one line and D, E, and F are any three distinct points on another line.

a) Draw $\overline{AE}$ and $\overline{BD}$. Label their point of intersection X.
b) Draw $\overline{AF}$ and $\overline{CD}$. Label their point of intersection Y.
c) Draw $\overline{BF}$ and $\overline{CE}$. Label their point of intersection Z.
d) Draw a line through points X and Z.

e) What did you discover about point Y? _____

_____

That the points X, Y, and Z are collinear is an interesting geometrical relationship that can be easily constructed with a ruler. The proof that the three points are collinear belongs to projective geometry and not to Euclidean geometry. This relationship was discovered by one of the last great Greek mathematicians, Pappus, around A.D. 300.

Basic Geometry   CONSTRUCTIONS: Geometric Patterns and Addition

Geometric Patterns and Addition

Interesting geometric patterns may be created by using arrays arranged like the ones below. A dot is placed with each numeral, and line segments are drawn to show equal sums. The dots serve as endpoints of the segments. Notice that the arrangement of the numerals results in a one-more and one-less pattern.

Give students the idea and then let them create and color their own patterns.

1. This array can be used for the basic facts for the number 11.

```
1       2       3       4       5
•       •       •       •       •


•       •       •       •       •
6       7       8       9       10
```

Connect 1 and 10, 2 and 9, 3 and 8, 4 and 7, and 5 and 6. Notice that 1 + 10 = 11, 2 + 9 = 11, 3 + 8 = 11, 4 + 7 = 11, and 5 + 6 = 11. Notice that if you start with the bottom row of numerals you illustrate the commutative principle of addition because 6 + 5 = 11, 7 + 4 = 11, and so on. The segments are drawn in the illustration below.

2. The same array may be used to give another pattern.

Notice that 1 + 7 = 8 and 2 + 6 = 8, 2 + 8 = 10 and 3 + 7 = 10, 3 + 9 = 12 and 4 + 8 = 12, and 4 + 10 = 14 and 5 + 9 = 14. The segments have been drawn to show these sums.

© Mark Twain Media, Inc., Publisher

Basic Geometry CONSTRUCTIONS: Geometric Patterns and Addition

Name _____ Date _____

3. Finally, if all of the segments are drawn to show pairs of equal sums, the following pattern will result.

Use the space below to create your own arrays.

Paper Folding

Paper folding can offer a wealth of ideas for helping students develop intuitive notions of geometry. Ordinary paper, waxed paper, newspaper, pages from magazines, and so forth may be used.

There are only three basic folds—one to bisect a segment, one to bisect an angle, and one to make a perpendicular from a point to a line.

1. To bisect a line segment, crease the paper sharply to make a segment as shown at right.

Then fold the paper over so that the ends of the segment coincide and again crease the paper sharply.

Unfold the paper. The second crease represents the perpendicular bisector of the segment.

This technique is used to find the midpoint of the side of a triangle or other polygon, to make a right angle, to construct the perpendicular bisector of the side of a triangle, and so on.

Basic Geometry · CONSTRUCTIONS: Paper Folding

2. To bisect an angle, fold the paper so that the two sides of the angle coincide, then make a sharp crease along the fold.

Basic Geometry   CONSTRUCTIONS: Paper Folding

3. To fold a perpendicular from a point to a line, first crease the paper to locate a segment. Then make a dot to represent a point.

— dot for point

— crease for segment

Now fold the paper so that the dot is on the fold and the parts of the line segment are over one another.

fold for perpendicular

point

This technique may be used to fold the altitudes of a triangle.

Basic Geometry								CONSTRUCTIONS: Paper Folding: Exercises

Name _____		Date _____

Exercises

1. Practice folding paper to make a segment and an angle, to bisect a line segment, to make a right angle, and to bisect an angle.

2. Fold a triangle.

3. Fold a quadrilateral.

4. Fold a rectangle.

5. Fold a pentagon.

6. Cut out a triangular region. Find the midpoint of each side. Then make folds over each pair of midpoints as shown. The dotted lines are folds.

   a) What discoveries can you make? _____

   _____

7. Cut out a general quadrilateral region. Find the midpoint of each side. Then make folds over each pair of midpoints as shown. The dotted lines are folds.

   a) What discoveries can you make? _____

   _____

   b) Compare the length of $\overline{AB}$ and $\overline{CD}$. _____

   c) Compare the length of $\overline{AD}$ and $\overline{BC}$. _____

   d) What seems to be true of ABCD? _____

Basic Geometry CONSTRUCTIONS: Paper Folding: Exercises

Name _____ Date _____

8. Cut out four different triangles to use in the exercises that follow.

   a) Bisect each angle of a triangle by folding. What seems to be true of the three angle bisectors?

   _____

   ← angle bisector

   b) By folding, locate the perpendicular bisector of each side of a triangle. What seems to be true of the three perpendicular bisectors?

   _____

   ← perpendicular bisector

   c) By folding, locate the three altitudes of a triangle. What seems to be true of the three altitudes?

   _____

   ← right angles
   altitude →

   d) By folding, locate the three medians. A **median** of a triangle is the segment with a vertex and the midpoint of the opposite side as endpoints.

   ← median

   The three medians should meet in a point, which is the **centroid** (center of gravity) of the triangular region. Use the triangle you have just made as a pattern. Cut out a triangular region from heavy, uniform cardboard. Mark a point to show the centroid you found. See whether this triangular region will balance on a pinpoint placed at the centroid.

© Mark Twain Media, Inc., Publisher

SPACE FIGURES

Space figures are sets of points that are not all in the same plane. Just as there are closed curves in a plane, there are closed surfaces in spaces. Among the common space figures introduced in elementary school mathematics are cones, spheres, pyramids, prisms, and cylinders.

Each of these space figures consists only of the set of points on the surface. For example, a basketball is a good model of a sphere, an empty chalk box is a good model of a rectangular prism, and an empty coffee can is a good model of a cylinder.

A simple closed surface is a set of points in space that separates space into three sets of points: the set of points **in** the simple closed space figure, the set of points **in the interior** of the figure, and the set of points **in the exterior** of the figure.

The set of points in a simple closed plane curve in union with the set of points in the interior of the curve is a **plane region**. A sheet of paper is a model of a plane region. Likewise, in space geometry, the set of points in a simple closed surface in union with the set of points in the interior of the surface is a **space region**. A tennis ball is a model of a simple closed surface, known as a sphere, while an orange is a model of a spherical region.

Basic Geometry

SPACE FIGURES

In **plane geometry**, we work with two dimensions: length and width. In **solid geometry**, we work with three dimensions: length, width, and height. Although the surface of a sheet of paper has only two dimensions, we can picture three-dimensional figures. For prisms and pyramids, the edges we can see are represented by solid marks, and the edges we cannot see are represented by dashed marks. For example, here are pictures of a rectangular prism and a triangular pyramid.

In order to describe prisms and pyramids, three special words are needed. The **faces** are the flat sides of the prism. A rectangular prism has six rectangular regions as faces.

The **edges** are line segments, each of which is the intersection of two faces. A rectangular prism has 12 edges.

The **vertices** (plural of vertex) are points of intersection of three edges. A rectangular prism has eight vertices.

Basic Geometry

SPACE FIGURES: Prisms

Name _____ Date _____

Prisms

Fold a sheet of paper lengthwise as shown in the illustration below.

tab

Next, make the sheet into a triangular tube, which is open at both ends, and secure the tab with transparent tape.

1. What is the shape of each side? _____

2. What is the shape of each end? _____

3. Stand the tube on end on a horizontal surface. Is it perpendicular to the surface?

_____

4. Do the two triangular ends lie in parallel planes? _____

© Mark Twain Media, Inc., Publisher   86

Prisms with bases other than triangles can be created in this same way by making more folds in the paper.

Imagine that the two triangular ends are regions and that the resulting figure now has five sides; that is, two triangular regions as ends and three rectangular regions as sides. This sealed, **empty** tube represents a space figure known as a triangular prism; specifically a right triangular prism, since the sides are perpendicular to the bases.

Only **right prisms** are to be considered in this unit. The lateral faces are rectangular regions and are perpendicular to the bases. In children's language, "They stand straight up and down."

right pentagonal prism

Other prisms are shaped so that the lateral faces are not perpendicular to the bases. In children's language, "They lean to one side."

prism that is not a right prism

Basic Geometry

SPACE FIGURES: Patterns for Prisms

Name _____ Date _____

Patterns for Prisms

1. This is a pattern for a triangular prism.

You may make models of this prism by tracing the pattern or making copies of this page and then cutting it out along the solid marks and folding along the dashed marks. Tape or glue the tabs to the rectangular sides of the prism.

a) A triangular prism has _____ triangular faces and _____ rectangular faces.

b) A triangular prism has _____ vertices.

c) A triangular prism has _____ edges.

© Mark Twain Media, Inc., Publisher

Basic Geometry   SPACE FIGURES: Patterns for Prisms

Name _____ Date _____

2. This is a pattern for a rectangular prism.

When the pattern is cut out and folded to make a model of a prism, it will look like a box.

a) A rectangular prism has _____ rectangular faces, _____ edges, and _____ vertices.

Basic Geometry

SPACE FIGURES: Patterns for Prisms

Name _____ Date _____

3. This is a pattern for a pentagonal prism.

a) A pentagonal prism has _____ pentagonal faces and _____ rectangular faces, making _____ faces in all.

b) It has _____ vertices and _____ edges.

Basic Geometry SPACE FIGURES: Prisms

Name _____ Date _____

The following table names and describes four kinds of right prisms. Complete the table under number of vertices, edges, and faces. Can you discover any pattern?

Kind of Right Prism	Parallel Bases	Number of Vertices	Number of Edges	Number of Faces
Triangular Prism	Triangular Regions	6	9	5
Quadrilateral Prism	Quadrilateral Regions	___	___	___
Pentagonal Prism	Pentagonal Regions	___	___	___
Hexagonal Prism	Hexagonal Regions	___	___	___

© Mark Twain Media, Inc., Publisher

Basic Geometry

SPACE FIGURES: Pyramids

Name _____ Date _____

Pyramids

Another kind of space figure is the pyramid. Trace or make copies of the following patterns and use them to make models of pyramids.

1. This is a pattern for a triangular pyramid or tetrahedron.

2. This is a pattern for a quadrilateral (or quadrangular) pyramid.

© Mark Twain Media, Inc., Publisher

Basic Geometry

SPACE FIGURES: Pyramids

Name _____ Date _____

3. This is a pattern for a pentagonal pyramid.

Pyramids are classified according to the shape of the polygonal region forming the base. For example, the following is a quadrilateral pyramid.

4. For a pyramid, the lateral faces are triangular regions. The above pyramid has _____ faces, _____ vertices, and _____ edges.

© Mark Twain Media, Inc., Publisher

Basic Geometry

SPACE FIGURES: Pyramids

Name _____ Date _____

The following table names and describes four kinds of pyramids. Complete the table under the number of vertices, edges, and faces. Can you discover any pattern?

Kind of Pyramid	Base	Number of Vertices	Number of Edges	Number of Faces
1. Triangular Pyramid	Triangular Region	4	6	4
2. Quadrilateral Pyramid	Quadrilateral Region	___	___	___
3. Pentagonal Pyramid	Pentagonal Region	___	___	___
4. Hexagonal Pyramid	Hexagonal Region	___	___	___

© Mark Twain Media, Inc., Publisher

Basic Geometry

SPACE FIGURES: Cylinders

Cylinders

The most familiar type of cylinder, and the one usually considered in elementary school mathematics is the **right circular cylinder**. The two bases of the cylinder are congruent circular regions that lie in parallel planes. A segment with the two centers as endpoints is perpendicular to both bases. Also, segments with corresponding points in the boundaries of each circular region are perpendicular to both bases.

Examine an ordinary tin can. Think about what the parts of the can must have looked like before they were put together. If you are not sure, get a can opener and cut a can apart. Actually, you can tell what the curved (lateral) surface would look like by making a perpendicular cut in the label on the can, peeling it off the can, and flattening it out. The can now consists of a rectangular region and two congruent circular regions.

A right circular cylinder is only one kind of cylinder. The following diagrams illustrate some other cylinders.

The bases, which are simple closed regions at the ends of the cylinders, are congruent and parallel. The surface or surfaces that join the boundaries of the bases are called the lateral faces.

Cylinders can have bases other than circular regions. The following are examples of shapes that the bases of a cylinder may have.

A right circular cylinder is the only one usually considered in the elementary grades. However, children may be made aware of other models of cylinders commonly found around the home. An ordinary sardine can, a plastic toothbrush container with oval ends, a rounded clothes hamper designed to fit into a square corner, and so on are types of cylinders.

© Mark Twain Media, Inc., Publisher

Basic Geometry **SPACE FIGURES: Cylinders**

This is the pattern for a right circular cylinder.

Basic Geometry

SPACE FIGURES: Spheres

Name _____ Date _____

Spheres

The geometric shape suggested by the surface of a ball is a **sphere**. A sphere, like the other space figures considered in this unit, is a closed surface. In children's language, "It is a hollow ball."

Exercises

1. If you slice straight through a hollow ball, what will be the shape of the rim of the cut?
   _____

2. Since a round orange is easier to manage than a hollow ball, use an orange for some experimentation.

   a) Slice the top off an orange. What is the shape of the rim of both pieces?
   _____

   b) Imagine that the orange is perfectly round. Every time you make a cut through the whole orange, what is the shape of the rim of the cut? _____

   c) Now slice through the orange so that you have the longest possible rim on the cut surfaces. What is the shape of the rim? _____

   d) In how many different ways can you slice through a whole orange so that you will have the longest rim on the cut surfaces? _____

   e) In how many ways can you cut the orange in half? _____

   f) How could you locate the center of the orange? _____
   _____

The above exercises were intended to help develop some intuitive notions of the intersections of planes and a sphere. If a sphere is cut by a plane, the intersection is a circle.

If a plane contains the center of the sphere, the intersection is a **great circle**. In the illustration, the intersection of plane B and the sphere is a great circle.

If a plane does not contain the center of the sphere, the intersection is a **small circle**. In the illustration, the intersection of plane A and the sphere is a small circle. Likewise, the intersection of plane D and the sphere is a small circle.

Basic Geometry

SPACE FIGURES: Spheres

In plane geometry, the shortest distance between two points in a plane is the length of the segment with the given points as endpoints. On a sphere, the shortest distance between two points is the length of the shorter arc of the great circle that contains these two points. Airplanes take the shortest distance between cities of the earth by flying on **great circle routes**.

To locate positions on the earth's surface, a grid is formed by drawing two sets of circles.

North Pole

South Pole

A set of great circles called **meridians** or **lines of longitude** are drawn through the poles.

The **equator** is a great circle whose plane is perpendicular to the diameter with the North and South Poles as endpoints.

A set of small circles called **parallels of latitude** are drawn with their planes parallel to the plane of the equator.

North Pole

Equator

South Pole

Basic Geometry

SPACE FIGURES: Spheres

These two sets of circles form a grid. A location may be determined by the intersection of a parallel of latitude and a meridian of longitude.

North Pole

South Pole

A sphere is a closed surface, all points of which are the same distance from an interior point called the **center**. A **radius** is a segment from the center to a point on the sphere. A **diameter** is a segment that contains the center and two points of the sphere as endpoints.

All radii of the same sphere are congruent. Also, all diameters of the same sphere are congruent.

Basic Geometry SPACE FIGURES: Volumes and Surface Areas for Specific Figures

Volumes and Surface Areas for Specific Figures

Recall all of the figures introduced thus far.

Triangular Prism   Rectangular Prism   Pentagonal Prism

Triangular Pyramid   Rectangular Pyramid   Pentagonal Pyramid

Cylinder   Sphere   Cone

Notice how the figures were grouped? All prisms were together, then all pyramids, followed by all circular figures. This grouping allows for ease in determining volumes and surface areas.

© Mark Twain Media, Inc., Publisher   100

Prisms

Recall that lateral faces were the parallelogram-shaped faces on the sides of the prism, and the bases were the polygonal faces on the ends. To determine volumes and surface areas of any prism, all we need to know is how to find the areas of the bases, the height (or length) of the prism, and the perimeter of the base. Let's look at a rectangular prism.

The area of the bases is just the length of the base times the height of the base as seen here.

$$B = b_1 \times b_2$$

The height or length of the prism is the distance from one base to the other base. Usually the height is given by the letter **h** as seen here.

The perimeter of the base is just the distance around the base or just the sum of the lengths of the sides of the base as seen here.

$$p = b_1 + b_2 + b_1 + b_2$$

Therefore, the volume of a prism is: **V = Bh**, where **B** is the area of the base figure and **h** is the height of the prism.

The surface area of a prism is: **SA = LA + 2B**. **LA** is the lateral area. The lateral area is determined by multiplying the perimeter of the base figure times the height of the prism. **B** is the area of the base figure. This means that the surface area of a prism can be written as: **SA = ph + 2B**.

Pyramids

Recall that lateral faces were the triangular-shaped sides of the pyramid and the base was the polygonal face on the end. To determine volumes and surface areas of any pyramid, all we need to know is how to find the areas of the bases, the altitude or height of the pyramid, the slant height of the lateral faces, and the perimeter of the base. Let's look at a rectangular pyramid.

The area of the base is just the length of the base times the height of the base as seen here.

$B = b_1 \times b_2$

The altitude or height of the pyramid is the distance from the base to the vertex of the pyramid as seen here.

The slant height is the height of the lateral face of the pyramid, denoted by the letter **s**, as seen here.

The perimeter of the base is just the distance around the base or just the sum of the lengths of the sides of the base as seen here.

$$p = b_1 + b_2 + b_1 + b_2$$

Therefore, the volume of a pyramid is:

$$V = \tfrac{1}{3}Bh$$

where **B** is the area of the base figure and **h** is the altitude or height of the pyramid.

The surface area of a pyramid is:

$$SA = LA + B$$

LA is the lateral area. The lateral area is determined by multiplying one-half times the perimeter of the base figure times the slant height of the pyramid. **B** is the area of the base figure. This means that the surface area of a prism can be written as:

$$SA = \tfrac{1}{2}ps + B$$

Cylinders

Recall that the lateral face of a cylinder was rectangular shaped and the bases were the circular faces on the ends. To determine volumes and surface areas of any cylinder, all we need to know is how to find the areas of the bases and the height of the cylinder. Let's look at a cylinder.

The area of the bases is just the area of a circle as seen here.

$$B = \pi r^2$$

The height of the cylinder is the distance from one base to the other base of the cylinder as seen here.

Therefore, the volume of a cylinder is:

$$V = Bh$$

where **B** is the area of the base figure and **h** is the height of the cylinder. The area of a circle is pi (π) times the square of the radius (**r**) of the circle. This means that the volume of the cylinder can be written as:

$$V = \pi r^2 h$$

The surface area of a cylinder is: **SA = LA + 2B**.

LA is the lateral area. The lateral area is determined by multiplying the circumference of a circle times the height of the cylinder. **B** is the area of the base figure. This means that the surface area of a cylinder can be written as:

$$SA = 2\pi rh + 2\pi r^2$$

Basic Geometry — SPACE FIGURES: Volumes and Surface Areas for Specific Figures: Cones/Spheres

Cones

A cone has a circular base that narrows and ends with a vertex at the top as shown below.

The cone is almost identical to the cylinder except that its volume is exactly one-third the volume of a cylinder and the surface is one-half the surface area of a cylinder. Therefore, the volume of a cone is:

$$V = \tfrac{1}{3}\pi r^2 h$$

and the surface area is:

$$SA = \pi r s + \pi r^2$$

where **s** is the slant height of the cone.

Spheres

Spheres differ from prisms, pyramids, cylinders, and cones in that spheres do not have base figures. Instead, the only dimension of a sphere that is needed is the radius of the sphere as shown below.

The volume of a sphere is four-thirds times pi (π) times the cube of the radius of the sphere:

$$V = \tfrac{4}{3}\pi r^3$$

The surface area of a sphere is four times pi (π) times the square of the radius of the sphere:

$$SA = 4\pi r^2$$

Basic Geometry SPACE FIGURES: Volumes and Surface Areas for Specific Figures: Exercises

Name _____ Date _____

Exercises

1. Find the volume and surface area of a triangular prism and a triangular pyramid with the following dimensions. To find the area of the base triangle use the following formula: **area = $\frac{1}{2}$ x length of base x height of triangle**.

   Base height is 6 cm, base length is 8 cm, the base hypotenuse is 10 cm, the height of the prism or pyramid is 12 cm, and the slant height is 14 cm.

2. Find the volume and surface area of a cylinder and cone with the following dimensions.

   Base radius is 4 inches, the height of the cylinder or cone is 18 inches, and the slant height is 22 inches.

Basic Geometry — SPACE FIGURES: Volumes and Surface Areas for Specific Figures: Exercises

Name _____ Date _____

3. Find the volume and surface area of a sphere with a radius of 25 feet.

4. Draw a regular pentagon with side lengths of 2 inches. Determine the area of this pentagon. Use the formula: **area = 1.720 x a²**, in which **a** is the length of one of the sides.

Now find the volume and surface area of a pentagonal prism and pyramid with this base, a height of 6 inches and a slant height of 8 inches.

The Five Regular Polyhedrons

A **polyhedron** is a closed space figure whose faces are portions of planes. Prisms and pyramids are polyhedrons. A polyhedron whose faces are all regular polygons and whose vertices are all alike is a **regular polyhedron**. There are only five different regular polyhedrons.

- A **tetrahedron** (te-tre´-hē-dren) has four faces, which are equilateral triangles.

- An **octahedron** (ök-te´-hē-dren) has eight faces, which are equilateral triangles.

- An **icosahedron** (ī-kō-se´-hē-dren) has twenty faces, which are equilateral triangles.

- A **hexahedron** (hek-se-hē-dren), also called a cube, has six faces, which are squares.

- A **dodecahedron** (dō-dek-e´-hē-dren) has twelve faces, which are regular pentagons. This is the regular polyhedron that is often used to make novelty calendars, since there is one face for each month of the year.

The five regular polyhedrons were known to mathematicians long before the time of Christ. Since all five solids were described by Plato, they are often called Platonic solids. However, they were known before his time, as well.

The tetrahedron, cube, and octahedron are found as crystals in nature. Although the dodecahedron and the icosahedron do not occur in crystal form, they have been observed as skeletons of *Radiolaria,* which are microscopic sea animals. According to Howard Eves, "In 1885, a toy regular dodecahedron of Etruscan origin was unearthed on Monet Loffa, near Padua, and is held to date back to 500 B.C."*

Patterns for these regular polyhedrons are given on the next five pages. Each figure may also be made from d-stix, or the pattern may be run off on a colored transparency and then cut out and assembled.

---

*Eves, Howard. *An Introduction to the History of Mathematics,* Revised Edition. New York: Holt, Rinehart, Winston, 1964. p. 70.

Basic Geometry — SPACE FIGURES: The Five Regular Polyhedrons: Tetrahedron

Tetrahedron

Octahedron

Basic Geometry SPACE FIGURES: The Five Regular Polyhedrons: Icosahedron

Icosahedron

Basic Geometry   SPACE FIGURES: The Five Regular Polyhedrons: Hexahedron (Cuble)

Hexahedron (Cube)

© Mark Twain Media, Inc., Publisher   112

Basic Geometry SPACE FIGURES: The Five Regular Polyhedrons: Dodecahedron

Dodecahedron

GLOSSARY

Copies of the glossary may be made and given to students to keep in their geometry or math folders or binders. Students can then use the glossary as a quick reference tool.

Acute angle: An angle whose measure in degrees is less than 90

Acute triangle: Has all acute angles (less than 90°)

Angle: The set of points in the union of two rays with a common endpoint

Arc: A subset of the set of points in a circle

Centroid: The center of gravity of a triangular region

Chord: A line segment whose endpoints are points on the circle

Circle: A closed plane curve with each point in the curve at the same distance from a given interior point called the center

Circumscribe: To draw a plane figure around another plane figure either to intersect each vertex of the inner figure or to have each side of the outer figure tangent to the inner figure

Collinear points: Three points located so that one is between the other two

Complementary angles: Two angles whose sum is exactly 90°

Concave figure: A figure in which a line segment with endpoints in a simple closed figure contains points in the exterior of the figure

Concurrent lines: Lines that have a point in common

Congruent: When two geometric figures are exactly the same size and shape

Construction: A geometric drawing in which points and lines were determined by using only two instruments, a straightedge and a compass

Convex figure: A figure in which a line segment with endpoints in a simple closed figure contains no points in the exterior of the figure

Coplanar lines: Two lines in the same plane; any two coplanar lines either intersect or are parallel

GLOSSARY

Diameter: A chord (line segment) whose endpoints are collinear with the center of a circle; the center is between the endpoints of the diameter

Dodecahedron: A polyhedron with 12 faces, which are regular pentagons

Edge: Line segments that are the intersection of two faces of a space figure

Equal: Two sets that contain exactly the same elements, or two numerals are names for the same number

Equator: A great circle whose plane is perpendicular to the diameter with the North and South Poles as endpoints

Equiangular triangle: All of its angles have the same measure

Equilateral triangle: Has three congruent sides

Euclid's Fifth Postulate: A given point not in a given line is in one and only one line parallel to the given line

Exterior: Outside a figure

Face: The flat side of a space figure

Great circle: In a plane that contains the center of a sphere, the intersection is a great circle

Hexahedron: A polyhedron with six faces, which are squares; also called a cube

Icosahedron: A polyhedron with 20 faces, which are equilateral triangles

Inscribe: To draw a plane figure inside another plane figure so that their boundaries touch at as many points as possible

Interior: Inside a figure

Intersection: Where two lines or planes meet

Isosceles triangle: Has at least two congruent sides

Line symmetry: When a line through a plane figure is such that it separates the figure so that the part on one side is an exact reflection of the part on the other side

GLOSSARY

Major Arc: An arc identified by its endpoints and a point between the endpoints

Meridian: A great circle of the earth passing through the geographical poles and any given point on the earth's surface

Minor Arc: An arc identified only by its endpoints

Noncollinear points: Three points not in the same straight line

Obtuse angle: An angle whose measure in degrees is greater than 90 but less than 180

Obtuse triangle: Has one obtuse angle (greater than 90°)

Octahedron: A polyhedron with eight faces, which are equilateral triangles

Parallel lines: Coplanar lines that do not intersect

Parallelogram: A quadrilateral with its opposite sides parallel

Parallels of latitude: A set of small circles drawn with their planes parallel to the plane of the equator

Pentagon: A polygon that is the union of the sets of points in five line segments

Plane geometry: Studies two dimensions: length and width

Polygon: The union of the sets of points in three or more line segments

Polygonal region: The union of the set of points in a polygon and the set of points in the interior of the polygon

Polyhedron: A closed space figure whose faces are portions of planes

Prism: A solid figure whose ends are parallel, polygonal, and congruent in size and shape and whose sides are parallelograms

Quadrilateral: A polygon that is the union of the sets of points in four line segments

Radius: The distance from the center to a point on the circle; it also may refer to the segment joining the center with a point on the circle

Ray: The union of a point and all the points in the half line to the left or right of the point; a ray has only one endpoint

GLOSSARY

Rectangle: A parallelogram with right angles

Regular polygon: A polygon with all of its sides congruent and all of its angles congruent

Regular polyhedron: A polyhedron whose faces are all regular polygons and whose vertices are all alike; the five regular polyhedrons are the tetrahedron, hexahedron, octahedron, dodecahedron, and icosahedron

Regular quadrilateral: A square

Regular triangle: An equilateral triangle

Rhombus: A parallelogram with adjacent sides congruent

Right angle: An angle whose measure in degrees is 90

Right circular cylinder: A cylinder whose bases are congruent circular regions that lie in parallel planes

Right prism: A prism with lateral faces that are rectangular regions and are perpendicular to the bases.

Right triangle: Has one right angle (equal to 90°)

Scalene triangle: Has no congruent sides

Skew lines: Two lines that are not coplanar; they do not intersect and are not parallel

Small circle: In a plane that does not contain the center of a sphere, the intersection is a small circle

Solid geometry: Studies three dimensions: length, width, and height

Space figures: Sets of points that are not all in the same plane

Space region: The set of points in a simple closed surface in union with the set of points in the interior of the surface

Sphere: A round solid figure having the surface equally distant from the center at all points

Square: A rectangle with adjacent sides congruent; it is also a parallelogram and a quadrilateral

Supplementary angles: Two angles whose sum is 180°

GLOSSARY

Surface area: The area or extent of the faces of a solid figure

Tetrahedron: A polyhedron with four faces, which are equilateral triangles

Trapezoid: A quadrilateral with one and only one pair of parallel sides

Triangle: The union of the sets of points in three line segments; it is the simplest polygon

Vertex (angles): The point of intersection of the two sides of an angle

Vertex (space figures): The point of intersection of three edges

Volume: The amount of space occupied in three dimensions

Use the space below for your own notes or definitions.

ANSWER KEYS

Line Segment (page 2)
You can only make one straight line to connect the two points.

Points—Lines—Planes: Exercises (pages 15–16)
1. [diagram]
2. [diagram]
3. [diagram]
4. [diagram]
5a. $\overleftrightarrow{RA}, \overleftrightarrow{RY}, \overleftrightarrow{AY}$
  b. $\overline{RA}, \overline{RY}, \overline{AY}$
  c. $\overrightarrow{RA}, \overrightarrow{RY}, \overrightarrow{AY}, \overrightarrow{YA}, \overrightarrow{AR}, \overrightarrow{YR}$ (any three)
6. [diagram]
7. [diagram]
8. [diagram]
9. [diagram]
10. [diagram]
11a. O
  b. ∠AOD
  c. $\overleftrightarrow{AB}$
  d. $\overline{AB}$
  e. ∠AOC
12. { }

Discovery Exercise (pages 17–18)
1. Teacher check.
2.
Plane	# of Points	# of Segments
A	2	1
B	3	3
C	4	6
D	5	10
E	6	15
F	7	21
	8	28
	9	36
	10	45

3. Teacher check. Accept a formula that conveys s = the sum of the number of points plus the number of segments of the plane preceding the current plane. For example, for E, add the points and segments for D. 5 + 10 = 15.

Congruence Pre-Test Activities (pages 19–22)
1. a. = j.
   b. = l.
   c. = k.
   d. = g.
   e. = h.
   f. = i.

2. a. = j.
   b. = l.
   c. = k.
   d. = h.
   e. = i.
   f. = g.

3. CD, EF

4. ∠XYZ, ∠DEF

5. a. = l.
   b. = m.
   c. = g.
   d. = k.
   e. = j.
   f. = n.
   i. = p.
   h. = o.

Congruence Exercises (pages 29–34)
1a. A circle
  b. Teacher check.
  c. All the points were the same distance from A.
2. Repeated congruent line segments are added together to get the desired length.
  a. 10 cm
  b. 3 in.
3. Repeated congruent squares are added together.

a. 12 square cm
4a. Yes b. Yes c. No
 d. Yes e. Yes f. No
 g. No   h. Yes i. Yes
 j. No   k. No   l. Yes
 m. Yes
5.
6. No. The three angles must add up to 180°. If you use a right angle, the remaining two angles must be less than 90°.
7. An equilateral triangle is also an isosceles triangle.
8. It is also equiangular.
9. A square is always a rhombus, but a rhombus is not always a square.
10. A rectangle is always a parallelogram, but a parallelogram is not always a rectangle.
11. A trapezoid has only one pair of parallel sides, while a parallelogram has both pairs of sides parallel.
12. No. A quadrilateral will have no parallel sides, one pair of parallel sides, or two pairs of parallel sides, so it cannot be both a trapezoid and a parallelogram at the same time.
13a. ∠A ↔ ∠Y ∠B ↔ ∠Z ∠C ↔ ∠X
     $\overline{AB}$ ↔ $\overline{YZ}$ $\overline{BC}$ ↔ $\overline{ZX}$ $\overline{CA}$ ↔ $\overline{XY}$
     △ABC ≅ △YZX

 b. ∠C ↔ ∠E ∠D ↔ ∠H ∠A ↔ ∠G
    ∠B ↔ ∠F
    $\overline{CD}$ ≅ $\overline{EH}$ $\overline{DA}$ ≅ $\overline{HG}$ $\overline{AB}$ ≅ $\overline{GF}$
    $\overline{BC}$ ≅ $\overline{FE}$
    Quadrilateral CDAB ≅ EHGF
14a. Yes
 b. Yes
 c. All are congruent.
 d. Answers will vary.
 e. Yes
 f. A triangle

g. Answers will vary. They should see a white chalice on a black background and two profiles in black on a white background.
h. They are line segments.

Area Activity (page 37)
All answers are in square units.
1. 54   2. 48   3. 75
4. 96   5. 18   6. 25
7. 51   8. 27   9. 36

Convex and Concave Figures: Exercises (page 40)
1.
2.
3.
4.

Lines of Symmetry: Exercises (page 43)
1. G = 0, E = 0, O = unlimited number, M = 1, E = 0, T = 1, R = 0, Y = 1
3. No, unless the paper is square.
4a. 3 b. 4 c. 5 d. 12 e. 16
5.
a.   b.   c.
d.   e.

Measurement of Angles (page 44)
1a. 50° b. 90° c. 110°
d. 130° e. 40° f. 80°

Measurement of Angles (page 45)
2a. 10° b. 90° c. 10°
d. 110° e. 61° f. 45°
g. 16° h. 60° i. 35°
j. 109° k. 170°

Complementary and Supplementary Angles (page 46)
3. ∠1 and ∠2, ∠1 and ∠3, ∠1 and ∠4, ∠2 and ∠3, ∠2 and ∠4, ∠3 and ∠4
4. ∠1 and ∠5, ∠3 and ∠4

Measurement of Angles: Exercises (pages 47–55)
1a. scalene, isosceles, equilateral
 b. obtuse, acute, right
2a. 180°
 b. The sum is 180°.
 c. The sum is 180°.
 d.

Angle	I	II	III	IV
∠A	66	69	42	43
∠B	46	38	48	107
∠C	68	73	90	30
Sum	180	180	180	180

Answers may vary slightly due to inaccuracies in measurement, but all the sums should be 180°.
The average is also 180°.
 e. 1) It equals 180°.
  2) m∠A = 60° m∠B = 60°
   m∠1 = 60° m∠3 = 60°
  3) They are congruent.
  4) They are congruent.
  5) The sums are equal.
3a. 60°
 b. 60°
 c. 60°
 d. They are congruent.
4a. 54°
 b. 54°
 c. 72°
 d. They are congruent.

5a. 2.25 in. d. 83°
 b. 1.85 in. e. 55°
 c. 1.5 in.   f. 42°
 g. The longest side is opposite the largest angle, and the shortest side is opposite the smallest angle.

6.

# of Sides	# of Ang.	# of Diag.	# of Tri.	Sum of 1 Tri.	Sum of Poly.	m∠
3	3	0	1	180°	180°	60°
4	4	1	2	180°	360°	90°
5	5	2	3	180°	540°	108°
6	6	3	4	180°	720°	120°
7	7	4	5	180°	900°	128.57°
8	8	5	6	180°	1080°	135°
10	10	7	8	180°	1440°	140°
12	12	9	10	180°	1800°	150°
n	n	n-3	n-2	180°	(n-2)180°	$\frac{(n-2)180°}{n}$

 a. The number of diagonals is three less than the number of sides.
 b. The number of triangles is two less than the number of sides.
 c. 180°
 d. It is found by subtracting two from the number of sides and multiplying times 180.
7a. 70°   e. 110°
 b. 70°   f. 110°
 c. 70°   g. 110°
 d. 70°   h. 110°
 i. ∠1, ∠2, ∠3, ∠4
  ∠5, ∠6, ∠7, ∠8
 j. Teacher check.
 k. 180°
 l. 180°
 m. They are supplementary angles, which total 180°.
9a. 90°
 b. Yes
 c. Yes
 d. Yes
10a. 30° b. 30° c. 150° d. 150°
 e. They are congruent.
11a. 60° b. 60° c. 120°

Basic Geometry ANSWER KEYS

12a. [figure: two parallel lines cut by a transversal with angles 147°, 33°, 33°, 147°, 147°, 33°, 33°, 147°]

12b. [figure: two intersecting lines with angles 134°, 46°, 46°, 134°]

12c. [figure: triangle with exterior angles 115°, 115°, and interior angles 65°, 65°, 50°]

Constructions (page 56)
The line segments are all the radii of the circles.

Intersection Exercises (page 57)
Points of intersection may be labeled with any letters.

1.
a. [two overlapping circles intersecting at A, B]
b. [circle with a line through C, D]
c. [circle with two intersecting lines through E, F, G, H, I]
d. [two arcs intersecting at J]
e. [two segments intersecting at K]
f. [triangle with points L, M, N]
g. [lines meeting at O, P, Q]
h. [lines through R, S, T, U]
i. [circle with line through V, W]
j. [two circles intersecting at X, Y]
k. [three overlapping circles with points A, B, C, D, E, F]

2.
a. [two overlapping circles]
b. [two circles intersecting with chord]
c. [two circles intersecting with line through both]

A. Construct a Line Segment Congruent to a Given Segment (page 58)
1. Teacher check.

B. Bisect a Line Segment (page 59)
1. Yes
2a. They are the same distance.
 b. Yes
3. Yes
4a–b. Teacher check.
5a–b. Teacher check.
 c. Yes
 d. Yes
 e. Teacher check.

C. Construct a Ray Perpendicular to a Line at a Given Point in the Line (pages 60–61)
1. Yes
2a–b. Teacher check.
3. Teacher check.

D. Construct a Perpendicular From a Point to a Line (pages 61–63)
1. Yes
2. Teacher check.
3. Teacher check.
4a–c. Teacher check.

E. Bisect a Given Angle (page 64)
1a–b. Teacher check.
2a–b. Teacher check.

F. Construct an Angle Congruent to a Given Angle (page 65)
1a–b. Teacher check.

G. Construct a Triangle Congruent to a Given Triangle (page 66)
1. Teacher check.

I. Construct a Line Parallel to a Given Line and at a Given Distance From It (page 68)
Teacher check diagram.
1. 60°, 60°, 120°, 120°
2. All four angles are 90°.
3. 60°, 60°, 120°, 120°
4. 30°, 30°, 150°, 150°

J. Separate a Circle Into Six Congruent Arcs (page 69)
1. Teacher check. Answers will vary.

Constructions: Exercises (pages 70–76)
1. equilateral
Teacher check triangle.
2. isosceles
Teacher check triangle.
3. Teacher check triangles.
   a. Yes
   b. Yes
   c. Triangles with congruent sides are congruent.
4. Teacher check triangles.
   a. Yes
   b. Yes
   c. Triangles with the same angle that have congruent sides to this angle are congruent.
5. Teacher check triangles.
   a. Yes
   b. Yes
   c. Triangles with two congruent angles and sharing congruent sides are congruent.
6. Teacher check square.
7. Teacher check rectangle.
8a. 4 in.
 b. 2 in.
 c. 5 in.
9a. 10 cm
 b. 7 cm
 c. 9 cm

10. Teacher check.
11. Teacher check.
12a–e. Teacher check.
   f. It is a right angle.
13a–d. Teacher check.
   e. It lies on line XZ.

Paper Folding (pages 82–83)
1–6. Teacher check.
6a. Answers will vary.
7. Teacher check.
   a. Answers will vary. The folds form a triangle.
   b. They are congruent.
   c. They are congruent.
   d. It is a parallelogram.
8a–c. The bisectors all intersect.

Prisms (page 86)
1. Rectangle
2. Triangle
3. Yes
4. Yes

Patterns for Prisms:
Triangular Prism (page 88)
1a. 2, 3
 b. 6
 c. 9
Rectangular Prism (page 89)
2a. 6, 12, 8
Pentagonal Prism (page 90)
3a. 2, 5, 7
 b. 10, 15

Prisms Table (page 91)
Triangular Prism: 6, 9, 5
Quadrilateral Prism: 8, 12, 6
Pentagonal Prism: 10, 15, 7
Hexagonal Prism: 12, 18, 8

Basic Geometry — ANSWER KEYS

Pyramids (page 93)
4. 5, 5, 8 (This includes the base.)

Pyramid Table (page 94)
Triangular Pyramid: 4, 6, 4
Quadrilateral Pyramid: 5, 8, 5
Pentagonal Pyramid: 6, 10, 6
Hexagonal Pyramid: 7, 12, 7

Spheres (page 97)
1. A circle
2a. A circle
 b. A circle
 c. A circle
 d. Unlimited
 e. Unlimited
 f. It is the intersection of the cuts that divide the orange in half.

Volumes and Surface Areas for Space Figures: Exercises (pages 106–107)
1. Triangular Prism:
 Volume = 288 cm^3
 Surface Area = 336 cm^2
 Triangular Pyramid:
 Volume = 96 cm^3
 Surface Area = 192 cm^2
2. Cylinder:
 Volume = 904.78 in.^{3}
 Surface Area = 552.92 in.^{2}
 Cone:
 Volume = 301.59 in.^{3}
 Surface Area = 326.73 in.^{2}
3. Sphere:
 Volume = 65,449.85 ft.^{3}
 Surface Area = 7,853.98 ft.^{2}
4. Pentagon:
 Area = 6.88 in.^{2}
 Pentagonal Prism:
 Volume = 41.28 in.^{3}
 Surface Area = 73.76 in.^{2}
 Pentagonal Pyramid:
 Volume = 13.76 in.^{3}
 Surface Area = 46.88 in.^{2}

Acknowledgment: The Illinois Department of Education.